A Survival Guide For Family Caregivers

Strength, Support, and Sources of Help for All Those Caring for Aging or Impaired Family Members

JO HORNE

CompCare® Publishers
Minneapolis, Minnesota

Published in the United States
by CompCare Publishers.

Library of Congress Cataloguing-in-Publication Data
Horne, Jo.
A survival guide for family caregivers / Jo Horne.
p. cm.
Includes bibliographical references.
ISBN 0-89638-241-9
1. Aged — Care — United States. 2. Chronically ill — Care — United States. 3. Caregivers — United States — Psychology. I. Title.
HV1461.H68 1991 91-15453
362.82 — dc20 CIP

Cover and interior design by MacLean and Tuminelly.

Inquiries, orders, and catalog requests should be addressed to:
CompCare Publishers
2415 Annapolis Lane
Minneapolis, Minnesota 55441
612-559-4800 or 1-800-328-3330

6 5 4 3 2 1
96 95 94 93 92 91

With respect, affection, and gratitude to the staff, clients, and family caregivers at St. Tim's Senior Daycare Center of Milwaukee, whose dedication, humor, comfort, and support set a standard for caring that was the inspiration for this book, and who "rescued" me more often than I ever let them know.

PART TWO—SPECIFICS

PART THREE—POSTSCRIPTS

Acknowledgments

This book has its roots in my personal story of caring for my parents. In many ways it is a tribute to their achievements as parents. The ability to cope and create solutions when none seemed available came from an upbringing that instilled in my siblings and me the originality, strength, and sense of humor to maintain a quality of life for our parents without sacrificing our own.

My siblings are also heroes in this project. Often in the pages that follow, the focus is on what I did, how I managed. But the success of our giving care was born of mutual respect for each other's commitments outside of caregiving, a trust that we could count on one another, a diversity of skills, and an unspoken understanding that our individual history with each parent might make certain tasks emotionally wrenching for one and easier for another.

As much a part of our caregiving team as anyone are the women who have cared for my parents for the last five years. Their dedication, sacrifice, and loyalty have been the foundation of our success. These women have enriched my life with their devotion to my parents and their friendship to me.

But the beginnings of this project (as for much of my work) came from my husband, Larry Schmidt, when he asked me to create a "newsletter" about the kinds of people best served in adult daycare. At the time—ten years ago—adult daycare was relatively unknown in the United States. Larry was beginning one of the first programs in Wisconsin. Even many professionals were unfamiliar with the concept. We needed a vehicle that would instruct as well as advertise. The newsletter became a monthly essay about people we were serving at the daycare center—the frail older person as well as the family caregiver.

Calls started to come in. Social workers, home care planners, and nurses called to say an essay had brought a lump to their throats while another had made them laugh. Organizations called to ask if they could reprint portions of a particular story in their newsletters. And as I wrote each new issue, my own appreciation and respect for older persons and their caregivers grew. Later, as my own caregiving role expanded, writing these stories reminded me that I was not alone, giving me strength and comfort.

When it came time to tie those stories together in the work that follows, my editor, Jane Resh Thomas, gave invaluable and sensitive criticism and contributed in many subtle ways to the shaping of this book.

Finally, appreciation must go to all those professionals and family caregivers who struggle constantly to publicize the need for and establish a system that recognizes the contributions of all caregivers. These people work against incredible indifference and apathy to create options that will make caring for our aged a vital piece of a health care system that works for all ages.

In this list I include businesses who have had the foresight to recognize the growing needs of employees for assistance in understanding options; advocacy groups who tirelessly prod the political system to not forget the chronically frail; media people who have the courage to print stories and do visual pieces about caregiving even when many in the business consider the subject too depressing to address.

And most of all, I salute the hundreds of support groups meeting in homes and public places across the country. Though they often struggle to survive in the face of poor attendance and a shortage of qualified group leaders, they are the foundation of what will be there to provide care when today's caregiver needs care.

Postscript

As I finished the editing process of this book, my father died. Ours was a hard-fought battle against sickness and frailty and for his right to live out his life in dignity, but the rewards—the moments shared in this book, among others—were worth it. I will miss him every day of my life.

JH

Introduction

My role as a family caregiver began, as many do, when I received a call at my home in Wisconsin about my mother's admission to a small hospital in Virginia. The diagnosis was congestive heart failure. She was in the intensive care unit, my father said, and I had never heard him sound so frightened. Mom had always taken care of him in that rural community in the foothills of the Appalachians where they have lived for over forty years.

I decided to leave immediately for Virginia for two reasons. First, I felt Mom would have a better chance at recovery if she were not worrying about Dad. The nearest hospital is thirty miles from their home. She worried about his driving, especially at night, and knew he would insist on being with her. At seventy-eight, he still ran his own furniture store and thought of himself as invincible.

Second, although I have siblings, we all agreed that my experience as the co-director of an adult daycare center for frail older people equipped me best to oversee Mom's care. I could accomplish more in a short time on the scene than by long-distance telephone calls. Once I returned home, my brother and sisters would step in. From the outset, we were a team, working together in spite of personality differences to coordinate the best possible care for Mom and Dad.

My first days were intense, but filled with pleasant experiences with Mom's medical team, who surprised me with the variety of their services. The young doctor who had first seen Mom at the local clinic had expressed astonishment that she was still on her feet at all. He admitted her to the cardiac care unit of the nearest hospital, and later to intensive care. So, by the time my plane landed, Mom was already in good hands.

Still, the possibilities for aggravation could have made the entire experience a nightmare. The hospital, for example, was in a different county from the one where Mom normally would have received services. I was afraid that we might become entangled in a bureaucratic mess simply because of the difference in county residency. The hospital social worker consulted the necessary agencies and assured me there would be no problem. Another potential difficulty was my acting on behalf of my parents with no official document legally permitting me to do so. Sometimes since then, my parents' doctors have been reluctant to deal with me directly even though they acknowledge my parents' inability to digest the information they need to continue functioning. This time, however, the physicians accepted me as a sort of "care manager" for my mother.

Although my mother's condition was not even stabilized yet, I immediately started planning her home care. I was raising issues that would not otherwise have come up for days or even weeks, but Mom's medical team understood that I would be there only briefly; I needed to make arrangements for the long-term care of both parents.

Their attitude about aging was one of the major problems. They had gone along accepting their changing health as normal, even when they became dangerously ill. They had all sorts of reasons for not keeping appointments with specialists who might have diagnosed problems in the early stages and thus avoided crises. To that end I made an appointment with the local clinic doctor who had first diagnosed Mom's condition, hospitalized her, and possibly saved her life.

Together we reviewed both of my parents' medical histories. He was able to tell me what he had observed; I was able to fill him in on things such as their propensity for taking over-the-counter medications without much thought of the side effects. He and I set up a plan for him to see my parents on a regular basis.

There was no opportunity to meet face-to-face with the heart specialist or the neurologist who came in from yet another hospital to evaluate my mother. I always seemed to be en route when they were making rounds. But I spoke with each of them several times by phone. In a rural area with a shortage of doctors, and especially specialists, the demand on their time was enormous. They were harried and pressured, and yet I found them patient and concerned. Both of them saw my seventy-six-year-old mother as a vibrant person who needed some help in getting back to a normal life.

Not everything, of course, was perfect. When my mother was found confused and wandering the halls of the hospital one night, the nurse told me that after all, my mother was getting up there in years and I had to expect these things. My mother is occasionally confused since her stroke a few years ago, but I was offended by the blanket reasoning that *anyone* her age would be confused. I had to bite my tongue.

And occasionally I found myself tiptoeing around egos, fearful that if I offended or pressed this person or that, I might not get the care I wanted for my mother. Also my parents were not the most cooperative people in the world. In the hospital my mother frequently told me she had never seen the doctor, refusing to recognize a woman physician. Once home, Mom and Dad refused any outside services, insisting they could manage alone. And to this day—six caregiving years later, when the doctor asks, "How are you doing today?", they tend to answer, "Fine," even when one of them is being admitted to the hospital.

Before I returned home I wrote out everything that I had done and found out, to inform my parents once things settled down again. I posted phone numbers, cooked meals and filled the freezer, and worked out arrangements with siblings to drive my father to and from the hospital until Mom could be discharged. My siblings and I held a family meeting to lay out a concrete plan of who would do what once Mom was home.

Were we just lucky enough to hit all the agencies and professionals on a good day and get what we needed? Were my parents living in an unusual geographic area where services are superior? Or did we simply have the knowledge to know what calls to make, what questions to ask, and what services to expect?

Certainly my experience with the system as an advocate for others helped a lot. But the truth was, I didn't know what to expect there—I had no experience at all with that Virginia system. What worked was educating myself as quickly as possible, by asking questions, seeking help, and appreciating the time and energy people gave me.

Today that all seems a long time ago. In six years, my parents have changed doctors four or five times (in rural areas doctors sometimes tend to stay awhile and then move on). They have each been hospitalized at least three other times for catastrophic illnesses, they have round-the-clock help at home, their money is running out, my siblings and I are beginning to burn out, and my parents still answer the doctor's question, "How are you doing?" with "Fine."

The work began for me with that first phone call as it may begin for some of you. For others, the call may be more subtle. You may be visiting Mom one day and notice that things just don't seem right. You may start to worry about Dad living alone. You may notice some erratic behavior in a spouse. And one day you understand that you have begun the process of giving care.

This is a book about coping with giving care. You will read about other caregivers (composites of real stories drawn from interviews and observations). You will get a lot of my personal viewpoint as a caregiver and as a professional who works with both older people and their caregivers. At times, I may appear to paint a fairly heroic picture of myself. Nothing could be further from the truth. This is the story of how I have coped. My brother, sisters, and parents would all tell it differently. Any success I've experienced is directly related to the presence of a large network of supporters, especially my siblings and the women hired to care for my parents. But building that network of support was something I planned, and it is a key to success in giving care over a long period of time.

My work at the daycare center has given me a special opportunity to view both giving care and receiving it. Sometimes it's going to seem that I am biased toward the older person. You're going to read a lot about how you need to "walk in their shoes" and be empathetic and patient and understanding, how you need to do your homework and get the services and assistance you can for *them.* Sometimes you might even find yourself asking, "What about me—my needs? My feelings? My life?"

The principal secret I've learned as both a caregiver and an observer is that those who cope best are those who are able to exert at least some control and understanding of the situation. That control and understanding grow from an acceptance of the fact that one can only assist another adult whose physical or mental capacity is severely limited. You are *assisting* him—*you are NOT living life for him.*

Caregiving begins when one adult needs another's assistance to cope with daily life. BOTH lives are affected, as are the lives of others involved with them. The majority of primary caregivers are family members. Getting even more specific, they are wives, daughters, and daughters-in-law. Sometimes the person receiving care is her own primary caregiver as well, usually an older woman who outlives her husband and has no children or other family available to help. In such cases, the person needing care makes decisions alone or with the help of professionals, about whatever care and services she needs.

Looking down the road, we might even project that, in the future, more older women who need care will have to provide it for themselves. An increasing number of women never marry, or they divorce, or raise few children or none. These trends increase the likelihood that many women (and men) currently in their thirties and forties will lack a familial support network when they need care.

It's important to keep such demographics in mind as we care for today's older generations. What will we need as we age? What services are missing now that could help? Who will provide them and who will pay the bill? We must understand that caregivers do more than provide personal care; they are also advocates and representatives. Many caregivers take strength from this advocacy role and often find the will to continue.

In the last decade older people and their caregivers have benefited from a growing number of options in services. Just a generation ago, there were basically two choices: stay at home or move to a nursing home. Nursing homes consequently got a bad rap; placement there was something to be dreaded, even feared. Times have changed. While a nursing home remains the choice of last resort, it is sometimes the best and most caring solution for a person who needs complicated physical care or rehabilitation and convalescence. While I will offer many ideas for alternatives, nursing home care in some situations is the best choice.

This book cannot anticipate every situation. Sometimes the solutions it suggests will seem hopelessly optimistic compared with your experience. Sometimes the best advice I can offer (and I will offer it again and again) is to talk out your problems with others who are in the same boat, who understand what you are going through even when they don't have answers either. Surprisingly, even if no concrete solutions exist, others' support makes you feel better . . . stronger . . . more able to continue.

As you will see (and as many of you already know) caregiving is just one of the roles you play. The stress and anxiety you experience may depend on how that role meshes with the rest of your life, and the effort necessary to maintain a balance and keep all the balls in the air without dropping one. One woman who was trying to juggle a job, a marriage, social commitments, and civic duties with the care of her eighty-one-year-old mother, expressed her frustrations in a list of wishes:

I wish . . .

I wish things could be different.

I see other people's mothers growing old with all the vim and vigor of a television commercial about the "golden years." I wish mine could be like that, like my friend's mother who, at the same age, still drives and attends her club and volunteers and goes on vacation.

I wish Mother didn't look to me for the living of her life.

I wish I could make her understand that I do care, that I don't mind helping her, but that I have other responsibilities. I've grown up. I've become the person she taught me to be, and now she seems to resent that.

I wish I were better at this, that I didn't feel every little thing so intensely, that I could be more practical, that I could talk to her.

I wish Dad were still alive.

I wish my siblings would help more without my asking and telling how. I wish I'd paid more attention a few years ago when Mother's symptoms began. I thought her forgetfulness, paranoia, and erratic behavior was just grief.

I wish there were some sort of health care system that worked, really worked. I wish I didn't ever again have to listen to someone who knows nothing about what it means to take care of a frail, confused, old lady who happens to be your mother, tell me how the old people in this country have all the money and are robbing the young of their future.

I wish there were some magic formula for getting all the help she needs. I wish I had more money. I fantasize a lot about winning the lottery.

I wish I didn't dread the thought that one day Mother might not be able to live at home anymore. I wish I'd never promised "no nursing home," or better yet, I wish she would at least consider other choices.

I wish I didn't have to worry about how all this pressure is affecting my marriage. I wish I didn't have to live with the fact that day by day I see my husband hating my mother more for what her care is doing to me.

I wish she would show some appreciation.

Sometimes I wish I would get real sick, not deathly, but incapacitated for a while so that there would be no question of my being able to care for her, just for a while, just to give me a break. Let somebody else worry for a while.

And sometimes—God help me—I wish she would die, not because I hate her, but because I hate seeing her live out her days this way, so unhappy, so lonely, so imprisoned. And yes, because it would be easier for me.

I wish I didn't feel so guilty.

I wish I could have my mom again, all the time, not just now and then. I wish I didn't have to watch her grow old and die. I wish I didn't have to look in the mirror sometimes and know that her face is my face.

I wish it could be different.

While it may seem that this woman is either very critical of her mother or very depressed, she is actually just being honest. Her outcry was not originally written for public consumption. It was a release for her, a place where she could think and speak the things that would seem terrible, especially to her, if spoken to another person. Even caregivers who cope extremely well think "secret thoughts" that pass across their minds from time to time, even the occasional wish that a parent might die. Such thoughts are neither bad nor scandalous; they are simply human.

In my work, I meet a lot of caregivers. I'm just lucky that way. These people are a constant source of inspiration and amazement to me. One night I attended a support group meeting for people who care for Alzheimer's patients. Although the group was small, I noted something that I have seen often in these settings. It seems that one member of every group has been giving care for a long time and has settled into a sort of lifestyle with caregiving at its center. And at least one other person is just beginning to realize what the term "caregiver" really involves.

At this meeting was a woman named Martha, whose husband had been diagnosed as an Alzheimer's disease victim five years ago. (And these patients are indeed *victims*—robbed and mugged and assaulted by this disease until they have no control over what happens to them.) The word *serene* came to mind as I watched Martha in her unofficial role as group leader. Yet I knew what conflicts and emotions raged behind that facade of serenity.

Here was a woman entering those years when most couples breathe a sigh of relief as the last child takes off from the nest, and begin to discover themselves as a couple once again. That will never happen for Martha and her husband, Daniel. For three years after their last child left for college, Martha cared for Daniel at home. In those early days, she gave him her emotional strength as it became apparent that he could no longer perform the work he had so loved. She was the villain when she had to tell him he could no longer drive the family car. She dealt with anger and disappointment as old friends called less and less often. She tried to be understanding when these friends said, "I just don't know what to say—poor Dan."

And in the long months that followed, Martha went out and found a job for the first time since she and Dan married. She enrolled him in a daycare center after she came home one day and found that he had turned on the gas stove and left it on. She coped with his night wanderings when he got up in the middle of the night, dressed, and headed out the front door "to go to work." She dealt with her children's fears and frustrations about their inability to communicate with Dad anymore. In the last months, she bathed and dressed Dan, spoon fed him, helped him in the bathroom and cleaned him up when he didn't make it in time. During the preceding week, she had dealt with her own pain when he no longer seemed to recognize her, referring to her simply as "that woman."

Daniel now lives in a nursing home, his disease so far advanced that he needs constant care. I applaud Martha for the courage it took for her to come to that tough realization that moving her husband to a nursing home was not an act of failure or an end to her caregiving, but an act of love born out of her constant desire to give him the best care possible.

I learned a lot from Martha. She is a survivor. She searches for ways of coping that work. Sometimes the situation required hard work; sometimes difficult decisions were called for; sometimes she was downright frightened.

Across the room from Martha sat Linda. For Linda, caregiving was a new and bewildering experience. She hesitantly spoke of her anger and her fear that it would harm her or her mother, for whom she was caring. Her eyes were wide with unasked questions and unmentionable fears. What was she letting herself in for? She and her mother had never been that close anyway. How could they live under the same roof? What would happen to her marriage? Her children? Her work? Her life? She struggled to find words that wouldn't make her seem some kind of uncaring, ungrateful monster. "I must get some rest," she said. "Should I name her illness for her or not?" she asked. *Help me,* her voice and face pleaded.

And in between Martha and Linda are all the others: people who care from far away, worrying whether they have done enough, whether the fragile structure of services they have organized can hold up until the next time they can get away for a visit; others who see that a relative is beginning to need some care and who wonder how far the need will go; and others yet who deny that they have any problem (though these last rarely come to support groups).

If you are giving even minimal care to an older or chronically ill person, you have joined the Marthas and Lindas of this world. In the midst of helping that other, you must recognize your own need for help and support. You needn't go through this experience alone, nor sacrifice your whole life. You have a right to your own life, regardless of whether you are spouse, adult child, in-law, or friend.

Three basic principles will help you to cope with your task. Do your homework, and be prepared. Anticipate, but don't project. And, take care of yourself.

The process of identifying your role as a caregiver, and your feelings about that role, is sometimes painful. But it is essential if you are to find constructive ways to live in the days and weeks, and sometimes years, ahead. It's best not to gloss over the difficulties of caring for another adult who may be your spouse or parent. The road is fraught with pitfalls for both of you.

This book is not one of the several available handbooks about practical care. This is a book about getting through the hard times and enjoying the good times for however long they last, whether a minute or an hour. And it does recommend practical steps that can make your task easier.

Because my experience and work has been in the field of giving care to aged parents and spouses, that is the subject of this work. However, many of the coping techniques and exercises will be helpful to anyone caring for someone with chronic, debilitating illness (AIDS, cancer, or multiple sclerosis, for example). I urge you to consider the entire book, even those chapters about particular relationships, which may seem directed to someone other than you. One of the hallmarks of a coping caregiver is her persistent search, even in unlikely places, for new ideas and new understandings.

Whether you are just beginning or have been giving care for some time, now is the time to stop and take stock of your situation. Is there room in your life for your current responsibilities? Is there room for more intensive caregiving in the future? Are you already sacrificing too much of your own life in your devotion to your relative? Are you making good use of services (often free or insured) that could assist you? These are the principal questions as you explore ways to cope with your role as caregiver.

ONE

BASICS

Chapter 1

What on Earth Is a Caregiver?

A caregiver (I never liked the word "caretaker," which sounds like the title for somebody who maintains a large estate) is anyone, in various circumstances, who provides some assistance (physical, practical, emotional, legal, or financial) to another person which the recipient cannot provide for himself. The assistance may be as temporary as a favor for a sick friend who cannot take care of some basic task such as shoveling snow or buying groceries. Or the assistance may be permanent, such as transportation for an older person who can no longer drive and must rely on other means of transportation.

There are many kinds of caregiving. An adult child may care for aging parents "long distance." A man or woman caring for a spouse may also work at a full-time job. A person who began occasionally filling in the gaps may at a later stage become a continuous full-time caregiver.

Frank, for example, receives a call at work from his mother. His father has fallen at home and broken his hip. Frank takes an emergency leave from his job in a city several hundred miles away and arrives at the hospital after hours of driving. There he speaks to the medical team, finds out his father's prognosis, assists in explaining the situation to both parents, stays with his mother that night so she won't be alone in the house, tours the rehabilitation centers where his father will convalesce, and represents his parents.

Frank is a *crisis caregiver.* It is an emergency situation that prompts his involvement in the lives of his parents. Once that emergency resolves and his father recovers, his parents will return to their normal routine with perhaps some adaptations, and Frank will resume his normal role as their son until the next crisis.

That second crisis might cast Frank in an additional role, like Sara's, as *occasional caregiver.* Sara initially assisted her parents during an emergency when her mother had a stroke and was incapacitated for a time. During her mother's recovery, Sara often went to her parents' home and cooked for her father, took care of tasks such as shopping and laundry, and kept tabs on her mother's rehabilitation.

When Sara's mother had a second stroke a year later, it resulted in permanent disability. It affected her mother's speech and paralyzed her right side. Although she worked hard in therapy, she was unable to recover sufficiently to resume her normal routine. Both Sara and her parents were adamant that they could manage, but over time Sara's role in her parents' lives became more complex. She went to their home almost every evening after work and on weekends. She cooked double portions of the meals she made for her own husband and children, in order to supply her parents. Gradually she found herself dropping some of the activities she had enjoyed with her family. She worried constantly, and spent many sleepless nights.

Both Frank and Sara are members of a growing class known as the "sandwich generation"—adult children with careers and families of their own who are caring for their aging parents. Sara is well on her way to becoming a *full-time caregiver.*

Another woman, Agnes, understands all too well the meaning of that responsibility. When she and her husband Jack retired five years ago at the ages of sixty-eight and seventy, their future seemed idyllic. They had time and money for travel. They enjoyed a full social life and the company of many friends. Their children's scattering across the country gave them lots of interesting places to visit. Then Jack began to have some problems. His memory seemed erratic. Once when they were driving home, he got lost within the city limits of their hometown. He gradually gave up activities he had once enjoyed.

Agnes had heard a lot about Alzheimer's disease—one can hardly age in America today without the prospect looming on the horizon. Some of their friends had suffered the illness, and both Agnes and Jack had mourned the loss of these bright, vital people who were still living, but not really alive in the same way. Agnes was afraid, but she knew she had to learn what she was facing. She insisted that Jack have a full examination. The doctor's diagnosis was that a series of small undiagnosed strokes had occurred over a period of time. These undetected "accidents" had permanently damaged Jack's memory and ability to function. If the mini-strokes continued, he would gradually worsen. At best, he would stay at his present level of functioning for some time.

Agnes and Jack did take trips again. They attended many of the same functions and activities they had enjoyed before Jack became ill, but now it was Agnes who drove and made all the arrangements. She watched carefully to make sure Jack ate properly and did not overdo. As the strokes continued to occur, Jack's competence diminished and Agnes shouldered additional burdens. She became his full-time, round-the-clock *primary caregiver,* and because the person she cares for is her husband, Agnes also fills the role of *spousal caregiver.*

Aside from the time they devote to giving care, there are other considerations for Frank, Sara, and Agnes. Frank and Sara are both *working caregivers.* They have jobs that demand their attention, jobs that are necessary to their own, their family's and perhaps ultimately their parents' welfare. In the weeks and months to come, they may increasingly be called upon to attend to caregiving at the expense of their work—either in time lost or in attention not paid.

Frank is also a *long-distance caregiver.* He lives in a different community, several hundred miles from his parents. Eventually his geographic location may further complicate his role as caregiver.

While Agnes is a primary caregiver, others give care to Frank's and Sara's parents. Neither adult child is present continuously; at this stage, that unceasing duty falls to the "well" parents. Agnes is on call twenty-four hours a day. She is primarily responsible for not only her own needs but Jack's, and probably will continue to be, as long as her own health holds.

Sooner or later, all three of our caregivers will need some help from other sources. That help may come from other family members. Frank's brother or sister-in-law may need to become more involved in their parents' care. Sara's teen-aged children and her husband may assume some care of Sara's mother. Agnes's adult children may assist their mother and give her some respite. These *secondary caregivers* are invaluable and often overlooked resources for the people who bear the brunt.

A third category of caregivers are outside the family circle, the friends and neighbors who can help only intermittently. The assistance of these *casual caregivers* is sporadic and occasional. A neighbor heads out for the grocery store, spots Agnes in the back yard and offers to pick up a quart of milk. A friend notices that Sara's father seems overwhelmed and offers to sit with Sara's mother while he takes a break. The primary caregiver for a family member, acutely aware of the role's pressures, may also be a casual or secondary caregiver for others—older neighbors, other relatives or friends.

These casual caregivers may underestimate the value of their kindness. Often they genuinely want to help, but do not want to become TOO involved. Because they cannot offer something major, they may not offer anything at all, and the primary caregiver may be hurt that no one seems to care. A friendly gesture, like stopping by for a few minutes to share a cup of coffee, may relieve the stress. Sending their teen-aged son over to mow the lawn or calling after two days of stay-in-the-house weather relieves the loneliness.

Finally there is an expanding community of *professional caregivers.* These are the nurses, physicians, social workers, and home health workers who staff the programs and institutions that fund and provide services for frail older persons. They include the people who deliver meals to shut-ins, who deliver mail and packages and newspapers, the drivers who transport people with disabilities.

Even if you are the primary caregiver, you do not have to do it all alone. Other people and services are available to help.

Which brings us to one last category: a *reluctant caregiver* is one who adopts the role by default because nobody else can do it or she seems the most logical choice. She may have neither desire nor aptitude for the task, but is thrust into it by factors such as marriage, parentage, geography, availability, or the choice of the person who needs care. While all caregivers are vulnerable, one who does not wish to perform the role in the first place is definitely at risk and in need of support.

A caregiver's slide into her role may have been so gradual that she hardly realizes she made choices as she went along. The daily demands upon her may keep her too busy to analyze her circumstances or consider her options. But you need to know where you are now as well as where you're headed before you can set up a plan for coping. It helps to define in a personal way your role as a caregiver. No one else's situation is quite the same as yours. Others come from different family histories and different backgrounds—economic, educational, cultural. Just as every other relationship is unique, so is every caregiving relationship. You two are different, from the rest of the caregiving partnerships in the world and from each other. Recognizing those differences and acknowledging the effects of your role upon your own well-being is where you begin to adapt and find new ways to cope, both of you.

Though it may seem daunting, the following questionnaire will help you in a number of ways: to sharpen your awareness of your particular situation; increase your knowledge of options, however limited; and set you on the road to clarifying your role and seeking solutions to the special issues of your caregiving. This exercise and others in subsequent chapters may be just the right step for some readers; for others they may seem too binding or even downright inhibiting. Even here you have choices—to do the exercises now, to choose those that seem most relevant to your situation, to return to them later, or not to use them at all.

Exercises in Coping

IDENTIFYING CAREGIVER ROLES

Which of the following defines you as a caregiver today? (Mark all that apply.)

☐ Crisis caregiver (your family member manages fine most of the time unless there is an emergency or some catastrophic event).

☐ Occasional caregiver (you provide one or more services for your relative on an irregular basis. For example, you assist with tax preparation, provide transportation to doctors' appointments, assist with major household maintenance chores such as changing storms and screens).

☐ Adult child caregiver (you are the recipient's son or daughter, or in-law; you may have a spouse and children of your own; in most cases, you have lived for at least part of your adult life in your own separate household).

☐ Spousal caregiver (you are married to the person needing care).

☐ Primary caregiver (your family member depends on you for regular assistance in two or more facets of his life; you function, for example, as legal or financial advisor, you make decisions that directly affect him, you act as his representative in one or more situations).

☐ Working caregiver (you hold a part-time or full-time position for pay that is important or even essential to your own economic welfare and perhaps that of the person who depends upon your care).

☐ Long-distance caregiver (you live at least an hour's drive away and provide much of your assistance by telephone, depending on other people to assist in caring for your relative).

☐ Secondary caregiver (your parent, sibling, spouse, or in-law functions as the primary caregiver and you offer assistance in specific or nonspecific ways).

☐ Casual caregiver (you are a neighbor, acquaintance, or friend of a person needing care).

☐ Professional caregiver (you work in the health field providing support and services to older persons).

Which of the following roles do you play in addition to the caregiving roles marked on the previous page? (Again mark all that apply.)

☐ Employee

☐ Employer

☐ Spouse

☐ Parent

☐ Homemaker

☐ Civic leader

☐ Volunteer

Next, identify all the ways caregiving does or might affect various facets of your life:

In addition to your "official" roles, you hope to make time for your own pleasures. List the activities in which you currently engage for relaxation or personal fulfillment. (Traveling, membership in a social club, hobbies such as reading or knitting, working out at a gym, etc.)

DISCOVERING SOURCES FOR HELP

List all of the types of assistance you personally give your dependent and note how frequently you provide each task. (Shopping, yardwork, financial help, etc.) If you provide care for more than one person, such as both parents and in-laws, chart each situation.

TASK	DAILY	WEEKLY	MONTHLY	OCCASIONALLY

List any assistance provided by other members of the family, who provides that service, and how frequently such help is given. (Example: assistance with finances, brother, monthly.)

List services provided by professionals or agencies and how often those services are provided. (Example: hot noon meal, Senior Center, twice a week.)

Of the following list of services or assistance, which do you expect your dependent will need within the next year?

Transportation	Meal preparation
Personal grooming	Laundry
Managing finances	Toileting
Live-in or day help	Companionship
Counseling	Change in housing
Social outlets	Legal assistance
Shopping	Assistance with mobility (walking, moving from chair to bed, etc.)
Help with medications	

FIGURING THE COSTS—FINANCIAL AND EMOTIONAL

How much money have you spent on giving care in the past year? (Include travel, time lost from work, expenses you may have paid directly such as bills for doctors or other care.)

How much time do you currently devote every week to giving care? (1-4 hours? 5-8 hours? 9-12 hours? 13-18 hours? 19-24 hours? More? How much?)

______ hours per week.

How much has your relative paid for her care in the last year? Is that likely to increase in the coming year? Can she afford increasing costs of care?

The involvement of the caregiver, the needs of the recipient, and the time required could increase over time. Given that likelihood, you need to consider some prospects before they become realities.

How long have you been giving care (even on a limited basis)?

How has your life changed since you began?

How secure are the alternate sources of help your dependent currently receives? (If your brother helps with financial matters, is his assistance likely to continue or does he see such help as temporary? Are there time and usage limits on professional services—for example, is home care permanent or affected by time and illness?)

How do you expect your role as caregiver to change in the coming year? (The role of a crisis caregiver, for example, may actually slack off after the emergency has been met. The role of an adult child caregiver may become more intense, especially if one parent currently functions as the primary caregiver for the other, should that primary caregiver die or become incapacitated.)

What activities in your life (or the life of your family) have already been curtailed because of the demands of caregiving? (You and your spouse may have decided to take family vacations closer to home rather than risk being far away when a crisis occurs. You may have changed jobs or given up some social activity in order to accommodate your caregiving role.)

What activities are you considering giving up or adjusting in the near future?

How has caregiving affected your own physical, mental, and emotional health?

This leads us to the very gray and difficult area of "feelings."

Mark all of the feelings that you regularly experience. (Star those that are associated directly with your role as a caregiver.)

stress
anger
resentment
guilt
fear

concern
love
contentment
confusion
anxiety

fulfillment
happiness
frustration
fatigue
pleasure

Describe in one sentence how your role as caregiver affects your relationship with other people in your life.

Spouse:

Children:

Siblings:

Close friends:

Coworkers:

Care recipient:

Mark statements that describe your current stage of giving care.

☐ Things are under control—I am managing well and see no real problems.

☐ I have some real concerns about where all this is leading.

☐ Specific problems require solutions. (When Mom needs someone with her all the time, who will that person be? When the money runs out, what then?)

☐ I resent the cost of caregiving to me, the losses in my own life.

☐ I need help and don't know where to get it.

☐ I know there are services available, but I don't know how to tap into them.

☐ She won't accept help from anyone but me.

☐ My job is being jeopardized.

☐ My marriage is being compromised.

☐ My children's needs are not being met.

☐ I don't have enough hours in the day.

☐ Other people seem to manage this just fine; why can't I?

Of the following coping mechanisms, which ones match your methods for coping in any crisis or ongoing period of stress? (Mark all that apply.)

hostility
isolation
humor
denial
sedation
avoidance
passivity
internalizing
perseverance
indecision
withdrawal
seeking help
adaptation
fantasizing
blaming self
blaming others
research
positive thinking
open expression of feelings
rationalizing
distraction
faith/religion

GETTING SPECIFIC ABOUT WHAT CAREGIVING MAY MEAN

Considering each caregiving role you have assumed answer the following questions.

Primary Caregiver

(Having determined that you are the primary caregiver, identify one or more secondary caregivers. If you are a long-distance primary caregiver, these other persons might be the "on-site" caregivers.)

With what tasks are you currently providing assistance?

Driving
Cooking
Shopping
Cleaning

Home maintenance	Laundry
Personal care	Financial support
Bookkeeping	Tax preparation
Insurance claim filing	Arranging for services
Medical care	Other:

List the persons (adult children, siblings, other relatives, friends, neighbors, coworkers, clergypersons) who might be willing and available to assist in even some small way.

If you are a spousal caregiver or a caregiving adult child, are there children or siblings who should be helping? What are their roles? Have they been defined?

If you are trying to do everything yourself, why are you?

Take a look at your own routine and schedule.

Are you married?

Do you have children living at home?

Do you work?

Do you have social or volunteer activities that are important to you?

List your weekly activities. (Include mundane tasks such as laundry, cooking, cleaning. Don't leave out pleasures such as your weekly tennis game, singing in the church choir, or meeting friends for a movie.)

Compare your list of current activities to the list of your relative's needs which you intend to fulfill.

Where do those two lists mesh?

What must you sacrifice in order to provide care? (The lists may mesh if you can cook for your own family and your mother at the same time. They may conflict if Mother is afraid to stay alone at night and wants you to spend every night at her house.)

List the tasks that you now do which someone else might handle, including the likely helper to handle it.

Talk to your relative's physician and find out exactly what the prognosis is over the coming year. How do you see the need for care escalating over time? What tasks might have to be added? Who will perform them?

Call your local office on aging or speak with the hospital social worker and find out what agency services might be available for your relative. List services for which your relative may qualify, even if that service is not necessary at this time.

Home-delivered meals

Meals at a central site

Chore services

Home maintenance services

Telephone reassurance services

Home aide, personal care services

Home health care, medical services

Legal or financial services

Transportation programs

Adult daycare centers

Respite care programs

Volunteer visitor programs

Other:

As you will discover, no one can do everything. On the other hand there are ways to reorganize your life (and the life of your dependent) more than you might think possible. Don't be discouraged as you try to figure out where caregiving fits. It is possible to be a good caregiver without forfeiting your whole life.

Occasional Caregiver

List the tasks with which you now assist your relative, even if only occasionally, to help him function somewhat more independently.

How many of the tasks on your list have been added in the last six months?

How many of the tasks are you performing more frequently than you did at the start?

Do you see a pattern that involves your being needed more often by your relative than before?

Crisis Caregiver

If your relative were to become suddenly and seriously ill, are you the most likely person who would be on call to help him or her through the emergency?

Has this happened before? How many times? How recently?

If you have given crisis care before, did your relative make a full recovery? Or was there a need for some occasional assistance from you even after the crisis had passed?

What is the prognosis for recovery this time?

Have you researched available supports and services in your relative's community in case help should be necessary?

Long-Distance Caregiver

How did you become the primary caregiver?

Might others who live closer serve at least in a secondary caregiving capacity?

Have you researched the availability of professional and community services and supports in the older person's community?

Do you have at least one professional (physician, social worker, home health nurse, geriatric care manager) you can contact there to assist you in arranging for care in a crisis or who can oversee the delivery of promised services?

Have you contacted your relative's neighbors and friends and alerted them to the possible needs, given them your phone number, and enlisted their help in some *specific* way when it was offered?

Reluctant Caregiver

Why are you in the role of primary caregiver?

If there seems to be no one else to fill the role, which resources in the community might provide some assistance?

What is the source of your reluctance?

How does your relative feel about your being the caregiver?

If you really feel there is no choice, what are your options for making the best of the situation? You will do yourself and your relative an enormous favor if you agree to counseling with a professional care manager such as a social worker or support group facilitator, at least until you feel you have a handle on what is involved.

Working Caregiver

What care must you give right now?

In what ways are those demands likely to multiply over time?

How will you fit caregiving into your life?

Has giving care affected your performance at work?

Have you spoken with your personnel director at work and explored the company's willingness to assist you in managing care for your relative? (A growing number of businesses offer help to caregiving employees in the form of information, on-site support groups, lunch-time workshops and seminars, etc.)

Spousal Caregiver

What is the history of your relationship with your spouse?

How has that or might that be affected by the need for care?

Are secondary caregivers (adult children, siblings, friends) available to assist you?

In what ways do you anticipate that the need for care may grow?

How is your own health? Will you be physically able to maintain your health and care for your spouse?

What is the financial picture?

Adult Child Caregiver

What has been your relationship with this parent?

Do you have siblings and if so, why are you the designated primary caregiver and what will their roles be?

What is the pattern of dealing with crisis in your family? for this individual? for you?

What are the other facets of your life, apart from caregiving, and how must you adapt them to your need to care for your parent?

All Caregivers

In this complicated world, families face increasing crises: marriages, for example, childrearing, mixed families after divorce, financial woes, and dependency problems. Are there any other crisis situations in your life right now?

Chapter 2

Walk Around in Their Shoes

Walk around in *their* shoes? Isn't this supposed to be a book about the caregiver? Aren't you looking for some support for all the hardship this role has cost *you*? It is, and, I hope, you are. But whether you have been giving care for a long time or are just beginning, you may need to take a fresh look at your dependent. Believe it or not, you help yourself by knowing his feelings and frailties.

I've been caregiving for several years now, beginning with other people's aging relatives, and then caring for my own parents hundreds of miles away. My two caregiving roles have allowed me to see things from both outside and inside, from the perspective of both the caregiver and the recipient.

The first time I walked into the adult daycare center my husband had opened, I was frankly terrified. My experience with people who were old and frail and needy was limited to the stories he had brought home from his job as a nursing home administrator for the previous twelve years. When he had asked me to come out and lend a hand with activities at the daycare center, I hedged.

"I'm not good at this," I replied, remembering how I had burst into tears a year earlier when we attended a program for mentally retarded youngsters. "I'm not sure I can get through it."

"You'll be fine," he said. It was a declaration of hope rather than certainty—no one knew better than this man that a commercial for the telephone company might make me sob.

The fact was, he needed my help. We were a couple just starting our own business in a field that was largely unproven at the time. The daycare center was his dream. He had supported me in my own adventures; now it was his turn. So I screwed on my brightest (and I'm sure, most frozen) smile and went to work.

The first person to greet me at the center was Alice. She had that wide-eyed, distant look of one who lives in another world much of the time. Her fingers, made clawlike by arthritis, clutched at my arm.

"Oh, you came and then she . . . but I told . . . up North . . . and we were but you came."

My cheeks hurt from holding the smile so tightly in place. What on earth had I gotten into here? I was thankful that a nursing assistant I knew eased Alice into the other room. I took a deep breath and followed.

The few clients who were gathered for the art project I was about to present waited expectantly. "Everybody, this is Larry's wife, Jo," the nurse told them.

"Hi," I squeaked, and they all smiled. At the time I remember thinking, *Thank goodness, normal people.* Today, having known the heartbreak and some of the joys of working with dementia patients, I think of Alice and her forgetfulness as "normal" within such groups, but then it was all new to me. My ideas about aging and senility were fairly stereotypical. It would take some time among these people before my consciousness would be raised. Today I find myself cringing at the mere thought of remarks such as, "Well, he's eighty years old—he's probably senile, you know."

I don't remember much more about that first day. I'm sure I made some mistakes, expecting too much of some people and patronizing others. But they stayed in my mind long after I had left the center that afternoon. On the drive home I thought about Alice. From the nursing staff I had learned a bit about her. I began to see more than the babbling old lady who had greeted me at the door. If I could hear Alice through the babble, I wondered what might she want to say?

Alice's story

My name is Alice, and it is spring. Flowers. Breezes warm on my face. No more piles of slush, only the gray spots on my mind that won't melt. Is it May or June? And if it's June . . . what happened to May?

Today my neighbor stops by for coffee. She talks and talks about Judy. "Who is Judy?" I ask finally. She looks at me with disbelief. "Judy," she says as if I should know. "My daughter . . . Judy." She looks at me as if I were crazy. I am not crazy.

It's my birthday. Eighty years. I think I hurt my daughter's feelings. She gave me another kit for making an afghan. "Not another afghan," I said without much enthusiasm. The real truth is that my fingers won't do what I tell them. Could it be arthritis?

Time passes. A week? A month? My daughter stopped by this morning. "You're still in your robe," she says without first saying, "Hello." She is often exasperated with me these days. "It's after eleven o'clock, and we're going to lunch. Did you forget?"

"No," I lie. I not only forgot—I don't remember ever knowing.

After supper my son comes to visit. Something is up—he never comes by on a weekday. I can practically set my watch by his visits—every other Sunday with Rita and the kids. "Got anything to eat," he says and opens the refrigerator. Inside is a mostly empty carton of milk, part of a tomato, and not much else. He turns to me with such a look. I see my own fears mirrored in his eyes.

Moving day. My daughter is taking me to her house. "You'll have your own room," she says, sounding like one of those overly chipper nurses at the hospital.

"That's nice," I lie. I want to scream at her to leave me alone—to stop stealing my things, my house, my privacy. I get into the car. When did she become my parent?

I wake. It is very dark. I am in my own bed, but where? The window in my room is over there and not over here. I need to go to the bathroom, but where is it? Everything seems turned around.

I am outside. How did I get here? It's dark and quiet and scary. I want to go home . . . can't find it . . . turn here? . . . no . . . a car . . . stopping . . . lights . . . voices. I am so frightened. Nothing looks familiar.

My son-in-law gets out of the car. With relief I stumble toward him.

"I want to go home," I cry. He takes me to his house. "No, home," I sob. "You are home," he says. "This is where you live now." I never liked him—never trusted him.

It is colder. The leaves are orange rather than green. Did we have summer? My grandchildren prepare for school. I hear them whispering to their mother, "I can't bring my friends here. How would I ever explain Grandma?" I am a stranger. I go to my room to dress and pack.

Standing before the closet. There are so many colors. Too many patterns. I cannot choose. So I cannot dress. I close the closet.

"Time for your bath," my daughter calls when she has seen the last child off to school.

"I don't need one."

"Oh, yes, you do. It's been days. Now please don't fight me."

Where is my right to choice, my independence, my right to the privacy of my own nakedness? Have I become a baby? Look, I walk, I talk, I have a brain.

I can't remember how the faucet works.

We go to the doctor. He talks to my daughter. I am there, but not there. He is young. I don't know him. There are tests—blood drawn . . . strange machines . . . quizzes . . . . "Who is the President? Can you count backwards by sevens from one hundred?" Why? I wonder.

Another strange place. So many changes. I am tired of changes. Why don't they just leave me alone? Let me go home? They're going to abandon me here. I've really made them angry this time. I've got to call them and apologize.

"Your daughter will be here at four o'clock," the woman in white tells me. She smiles and pats my arm. *Oh, no, she won't,* I scream silently. I have been left here to die.

Four o'clock and she walks through the door. "Here's your daughter," the one in white says. Celebration! I am not to be left. It was another test, and this time I passed.

Again the strange place—daycare, the sign says. Here is lunch. I reach for my purse—no money. How embarrassing! I can't pay. I refuse the lunch . . . better than letting them know I can't pay.

"Eat," they urge. I try a little, but leave most of it. After lunch, no one comes for money. I clear and wipe the tables, just in case. I wish my daughter would let me help. It feels good—like old times.

Today is black and stormy to match my mood. Things are terrible at that place where I'm living. Everyone was angry this morning—even the young ones. And they were all angry at me! Why? And here it isn't much better. These women who sit at my table are talking . . . about me maybe. Now here comes that one with the crafts again. I can't do it, and she knows it—they're all just trying to embarrass me. I'll get my coat and leave.

"Alice?" A voice behind me.

I turn defiantly hanging on to my coat. I am leaving. "I can't because when Nancy, and if I go there and she, she'll just be so. . . ." Damn. It doesn't work—my mind doesn't work.

"I can see how upset you are," the woman says and I believe her. She looks right at me. She seems to understand.

"You're having a bad day, aren't you, Alice?"

The tears form. I am a grown woman—this girl could be my child. "No," I say and mean yes. "Thanks, but then if you, and I'll, and we'll just have to." Oh my God, I am crazy. Nothing works anymore.

"Alice? Would you mind sitting with me while I have a cup of coffee? You see, I'm not having a great day myself and it would really help."

I look at her. She has called me Alice—she knows who I am—she sees me . . . not some crazy lady . . . me—Alice.

As the days passed and I spent more time at the center, I looked at Alice differently and, in a way, we learned to communicate. I think perhaps it was her eyes. They were pale blue and for all their staring into a distant past I could not enter, they were lively and alert. And now and then, they focused directly on me, as if what I had just said she had somehow understood.

Alice made me think. What would it be like to be trapped in a mind where you clearly had something to say, but could not say it, where thought processes went on, but made no sense, where you had no recent past and no future, only this moment right now and all those old comforting memories of the years ago? And even if you still had your mind, would it be any better to be trapped in a body that was paralyzed by stroke or bent and gnarled by arthritis or slave to diabetes, emphysema, cancer, heart disease?

And what if there were no catastrophic event to set this decline in motion? What about those for whom aging is a slow process of loss—loss of mobility, loss of friends, loss of social contact, loss of job? In the early stages of disability there may still be possibilities, but the future is not always certain. For some, I realized, aging is a daily process of choices and the lack of them. Like choices Hannah makes every day.

Hannah's story

It's a lovely day. I can see from my window. A young woman at the next apartment building is hanging clothes from a line on her balcony. I remember when we had the house. I used to love the smell of clothes fresh from drying outdoors.

I can't stretch my arm to reach a glass off the shelf. How could I possibly hang clothes again, even if I had a balcony?

There's the bell. Charlie, my mailman, taps out the familiar code. "Coming, Charlie," I call, knowing he will wait patiently for me to make my way to the door. Charlie comes by every day, whether I have mail or not, just to be sure I'm still kicking. I wish it were colder today. When it turns cold, I can usually persuade Charlie to come in for a cup of coffee and one of my sticky buns. "Nothing today, Mrs. Hawkins. Everything okay?"

I have made him wait several minutes while I struggled out of that club chair by the window. I'll have to remember either to stand by the door or sit on a straight chair until he comes. Here he is wasting all this time with me and there's not even any mail to deliver here.

I send Charlie on his way. As long as I'm up, I may as well try to do a few things. I'd like to tackle some fall cleaning. The holidays are coming. Perhaps I could ask Charlie and his family to come by for a visit. I'll have to make do with this broom—I just can't manage that heavy vacuum cleaner anymore. That dining room table could stand a good waxing.

But remember the last time you tried waxing it? You barely got one corner done before your elbow cried out against the motion of rubbing the shine.

Almost time for my soap opera. I'll just get my knitting and settle in. Got to get these sweaters made for the grandchildren; they expect one after all these years. I hope they fit. I haven't seen the kids in two years—living out there in California now. How the children grow.

I wish I could do more for them than just a sweater, but with my Social Security, I just can't afford more. Thank heavens for the years of knitting that have left me with all this extra yarn.

Wouldn't you know? Just settled in, and I have to go. Shouldn't have had that second cup of coffee this morning. Will I make it in time? Who knows? Lately my record has been awful. Can't stand this chair anyway—it's like trying to get out of quicksand.

I'm glad no one is here to see how clumsy I am. I'm glad no one will know if I don't make it to the bathroom in time. Of course, I'll know I didn't make it. . . .

Noon, and Caroline has come with my Meals-on-Wheels delivery. She's always so cheerful, but rushed. No time to stay and visit. More meals to deliver. People waiting. Still, it gets so lonely, eating alone most of the time.

I don't know when I last went to visit somebody. I'd like to go out, but even with an elevator in the building there are still those eight steps out front. Besides, I've been hearing some terrible stories about things that are happening right in this neighborhood in broad daylight.

Lunch is good. I have trouble chewing the meat, though, with my loose dentures. I mentioned that to the doctor, but he said new dentures would cost a lot. I don't see why they can't just fix the ones I have now. Oh look, there's a lovely baked apple and ice cream. I'll save that for later.

I thank God for agencies like this meal program. With my children out of town, this is like a lifeline. Still, the paper is filled with news of budget cuts and funding for such programs could be cut back. What will happen then? How will they choose who gets and who doesn't?

The phone sounds loud in this quiet apartment. I had almost dozed off. It's the hospital social worker—the one I met when I was in there for my heart. She's calling to say my friend Ellie has had a mild heart attack. Ellie listed me as someone who should be called. Ellie and I talk once a day, and she knew I would worry. The social worker says Ellie is really very frightened and, since she has no one else, would really like to see me. Can I come?

My mind reels with the enormity of the task of getting to the hospital. I cannot afford a cab—it is too far to the end of the month for that. But I am all Ellie has, and I will not let her down.

It takes me over an hour to get from my apartment to the hospital only a mile away. In the old days I would have simply walked the distance. But now tackling those front stairs is my first challenge. I manage with my cane and the handrail, but I am terrified through it all that I will fall. By the time I reach the bus stop, my heart is pounding. When the bus comes, several people have gathered at the stop. They rush ahead as soon as the driver opens the door. By the time it is my turn to board, no front seats are left.

Pausing to deposit my coins, I ask the driver to confirm my directions for getting to the hospital. He mutters an answer I cannot hear, and the bus lurches forward. I stumble my way to the nearest seat—halfway back. No one offers to help.

No one even looks at me. By the time I plop down, I am quite breathless and feeling awkward and old. Where is that sure-footed young woman who lives in my head?

At the hospital I have my choice between two low steps or a long winding ramp built for wheelchairs. I choose the steps. I see Ellie, and her relief at my visit is enough to make the struggle worthwhile. I remind her that there is a phone next to her bed and that she can call me anytime.

She is like a little girl, clutching my hand, her eyes wide with anxiety. I remember when I was here with my heart. My children flew in for a few days but had to get back to their jobs . . . to their lives. Ellie has no children. She is depending on me and that responsibility makes me stronger.

Leaving the hospital, I am more sure of myself. Now I know where I am going. I know what to expect. On the bus ride home, I find a seat in the front. I look around and enjoy the outing. I see a movie house playing something with Katherine Hepburn. She's my favorite, and I am tempted to get off the bus and see if I can make a matinee.

But of course, it would be dark when I came out, and I don't know the bus schedule. And besides, who can afford a movie?

By the time I reach home, I am thoroughly exhausted. My knee throbs as I climb the front stairs, and I feel generally lightheaded and a little sick as I wait for the elevator.

What if I had a heart attack? Who would know? Last time I was lucky. It happened right in the doctor's office. Of course, Charlie would know. But he won't bring the mail again until tomorrow. I'll be all right. After I get to my apartment, after my bath, I'll eat my baked apple and the ice cream.

A bath used to be such a pure pleasure. Now it is a chore to dread. The sides of the tub are high and it's hard to control the water temperature in these old buildings. What if I fell? My feelings of independence—so energizing this afternoon—wash away. As I dry myself, I see in the mirror not the reflection of what I feel like most of the time, but rather the image of what I am—old and frail and basically alone.

Your story

Think about Alice for a moment. In her imaginary monologue, she is confronting many changes in her life. While careful reading shows that these changes have occurred over a period of time, they may seem sudden to Alice, all happening at once. Consider how many of the changes entail some loss—loss of memory, loss of home, loss of independence, loss of control.

And for Hannah, in the second scenario, you might have many answers. Why doesn't she make friends with others in her building? Why doesn't she call old friends? Why doesn't she get a different chair, for heaven's sake? But she, too, often feels she cannot control her own destiny. Things seem to be in the hands of others. Activities she once took for granted are no longer possible. That can be very disturbing, debilitating even when there is no impairment. For Hannah, that loss is coupled with a weakened body wracked with arthritis and heart disease.

Your ability to understand—to walk around in your dependent's shoes—will help you to cope. I am not equating understanding with giving in, nor implying that you don't deserve the same understanding. As much as you need that understanding, you may not get it from the person you are caring for. If you can see your mother's perspective, at least you may be able to figure out where your tactics need to change. Sometimes, no matter how reasonable your idea may seem to you, it is just not acceptable to her.

For example, Mom has been rattling around in that big old house where you grew up ever since Dad died. She can't possibly keep up with the cleaning and maintenance, and the taxes alone are eating up her small income. You see one of these lovely new complexes that offers housekeeping and activities; the place even offers transportation. What could be better for your mom? But she adamantly refuses even to go and look at the place.

What's going on here? All you want is the best for Mom—a better life that would be less lonely and more secure. She's really a prisoner in that house, since she doesn't like to drive and most of her friends have either died or moved from the neighborhood. Why can't you make her see? When you talk to her, you get vague answers such as, "It's too expensive," or "I don't know anyone there." Never mind that she knows barely anyone in her own neighborhood well enough to say more than "Hello."

So you imagine yourself in your mother's shoes. What is so threatening about a move that clearly would ease her life? Think about Mom's recent history—Dad's death, the loss of friends, the gradual loss of social opportunities, her gradual withdrawal into the house. Is she perhaps clinging to the house because of what it represents to her? A time when she was happier? A time when life was smoother, a time when she was independent and in control? Is that house a vital piece of her identity?

And what might Mom's generation really think of senior apartment complexes? In her day you had two choices: die at home or in a nursing home. She's seen others move their parents under the guise of "doing what's best," when what they intended was a move to a nursing home. Mom doesn't want that. You keep talking about activities and nursing care available through the apartment complex; that may sound a lot like a nursing home to her. Keep in mind that, for people of her generation, nursing homes were to be avoided at all costs. She has no frame of reference for the changes that have occurred in the last decade which have made nursing homes just one of many specialized options for care.

Besides, the house is bought and paid for. Why should she shell out all that money every month to some landlord? And what if they go out of business—where is all her money then? Yes, money is tight, but at least she owns the roof over her head.

Realistically Mom may know that staying in the house under the current circumstances may not be the best idea. If truth be told, she is often frightened of noises she hears at night. But still she resists. You may need to examine your presentation of this idea of moving—are you *telling* her or discussing the idea with her? Is she clearly in control (assuming she is capable of making her own decisions)? Are other alternatives possible, such as sharing her own home with someone else—a college student or single adult who might do some housework or maintenance chores in exchange for a cheaper rent? Have you recently been making a number of decisions for her . . . perhaps even at her own request?

It is imperative that you learn to recognize what is actually going on—in your own stress and in your relative's—and not just name the symptoms. What's really going on when Mom refuses to move? The refusal is a symptom. The reasons *WHY* she won't consider the idea are the crux of the matter, and that's what you need to understand. What's really going on when you throw up your hands and shout, "I can't do this anymore"? Throwing up your hands and shouting are symptoms. *WHY* can't you do this anymore? If you can answer that question in very specific and honest terms, you will be on your way to coping with this particular crisis.

Without knowing details about the two people in this scenario, no one can offer real answers. The point is that looking at the issue from both perspectives, yours and your relative's, is vital to the caregiving process. Even when she has a mental impairment, she may still have some very strong feelings about certain issues, and none is more volatile than HOME.

So, how do you "try on" your relative's feelings? Use the following exercises to help you get started, and then from time to time, especially when you feel as if she is being stubborn just to spite you, stop and take a moment to "try on" those feelings again.

EXERCISES IN COPING

A WALK IN THOSE SHOES

How would you feel if . . .

you were driving or walking along and suddenly could not remember how to get home?

you could not remember the names of your children?

you made mistakes at work that you never used to make before?

you could not figure change for a five-dollar bill?

you could not remember reading the newspaper this morning?

you could make no sense of what you read?

you checked into a motel on vacation and the following morning could not remember coming there?

How would you feel if . . .

you could no longer drive?

you had to depend on others to help you to and from the bathroom?

you could not always control your bladder?

you had to wear diapers?

you had to eliminate foods from your diet you had always enjoyed?

you could no longer see to read?

you had to ask people to keep repeating themselves?

you had to depend on others for things you used to do for yourself?

How would you feel if . . .

you knew what you wanted to say, but could not put the words together?

your mind worked fine but your stroke had left you with aphasia and you could not speak in more than grunts and whimpers?

other people talked about you as if you weren't in the same room?

other people suddenly started to call you by childlike nicknames?

other people cooed and squealed over the most mundane accomplishment that you managed?

other people shouted at you, assuming you were deaf simply because you are old?

other people talked to you in slow, measured tones, as they would to a child because they assumed you could not understand?

other people kept telling you not to worry about anything, that everything will be taken care of for you?

If you really want to get inside your dependent's skin, simulate the impairments.

If he uses a wheelchair, try spending one hour in it while he is sleeping or not using it. Don't just sit there, do the things that you would normally do.

If she has a visual impairment, cover your eye or smear a petroleum jelly on sunglasses and then try to go about your normal routine.

If his hand and arm are paralyzed, try strapping down one of your own arms for the morning while you do your ordinary work. If it is his writing and eating hand that is paralyzed, be sure to "handicap" your own primary hand, and then try writing a note and eating a regular meal.

If she seems to have trouble with tasks that involve some dexterity, live and work for a few hours in ski mittens.

If she's confused, her state of mind will be hard to simulate. One way is to try some of the basic memory tests in your library. You may panic at first when you try these tests and realize how poorly you performed. (Most people do much worse than they think they should.) It will give you a small sense of the growing anxiety the mentally impaired person may feel when she is still fairly aware.

In general, use your imagination. Watch your relative as he goes through a day. What might life feel like to him? What are the stumbling blocks? What would you have trouble dealing with? Are there reasons he doesn't do as you suggest?

And by the way, it would not be a bad idea to let the person know you are trying these exercises, especially if he is mentally alert, but physically impaired. Your willingness to consider what it feels like to be in his shoes might spark his understanding of your own position.

Take some quiet time (five minutes—nothing major), and list the events that have led to the care you are giving.

1. Mom gave up driving.
2. Dad died.
3. Mom withdrew.
4. Mom had stroke.
5. Mom moved in with me.

Next to each item write the losses your relative might have experienced at that event:

1. Mom gave up driving. (Loss of independence.)
2. Dad died. (Loss of closest friend, helpmate, role in life.)
3. Mom withdrew. (Loss of social outlets, friends.)
4. Mom had stroke. (Loss of physical ability and speech.)
5. Mom moved in. (Loss of ownership; loss of possession; loss of power.)

Now think about each event and how it must have affected your relative emotionally. Even though your mother may have had some choice and control along the way, she had little or no control over some of the major events in her life. At first glance it may seem that she could have controlled her withdrawal after the death of her husband, but perhaps not. If you have ever been through a divorce or seen friends go through one, you've seen the social circle dissolve. When your mother's husband died, her friends, especially if they were still mostly couples, may have slowly drifted away. She may have participated in their withdrawal when she refused to seek their help or assistance, not wanting to be a bother.

Even if her social circle remained loyal through the mourning process, how did they deal with her stroke, and how are they adjusting to her new lifestyle, living with you? Sometimes people think they are doing a favor both for you and your chronically ill dependent by staying away. "Oh, they have so much to deal with already," friends may think; "the last thing they need is company popping in." They may be just plain ignorant and assume that a stroke or other chronic illness is tantamount to a death sentence. "Poor Ruth—I understand she just sits there in her wheelchair all day," they may say, assuming that Ruth chooses just to sit or is so senile as a result of the stroke that she has no choice. Which brings us full circle back to Alice and the subject of senility. Whether you are caring for someone who has Alzheimer's disease or for someone with occasional dementia caused by other conditions, you need to understand that the word "senile" does not mean "crazy." Although "senility" originates in a word that means "old," the condition is not inevitable in aging people. Remind yourself of the many older people, some well into their eighties and nineties, who function at a high intellectual level for all the days of their lives. Dementia can sometimes be reversed (or at least treated), but sometimes cannot. In either case, you need to keep in mind that your relative is an individual; those characteristics that made her unique in the past are still present, at least to some degree.

Taking that awareness a step further, look at the person with a physically debilitating condition and know that the same is true. He is a person, with a history and a relationship to you and others that cannot be erased by chronic illness. It may sometimes complicate your job as a caregiver to keep reminding yourself that once this man ran a company of 500 employees or this woman founded the local branch of the NAACP, but it will also make your association in their declining years more interesting and challenging.

Chapter 3

Facing Old Age

It finally happened. A friend who has been (and, of course, will always be) younger than I turned forty. At the risk of sounding uncharitable and less noble than I'd like to be, I have to admit that her birthday gave me great pleasure. Now she was no longer one of "them"—she had become one of "us." I took some unseemly delight when she did not move around the tennis court quite as nimbly on the day after turning the big four-o. I nodded knowingly when she mentioned she just didn't seem to have her usual stamina.

But my satisfaction was short-lived. For if she had become one of "us," who was US? We have arrived at the dreaded place of *middle-age.* We of the "don't-trust-anyone-over-thirty" generation never got around to exploring how we felt about those over forty . . . or . . . fifty or. . . . Another friend, a teacher, got into a discussion one day with her students and kiddingly asked them to guess her age. They agreed on thirty-six, and, at forty years, she was horrified. "Why?" I asked, thinking that I would have been thrilled. "Because," she moaned, "I thought they would say *twenty*-six."

It's true. As I move through each day, plan my life, think about the things I want to do, I view my future with the mindset of someone years—even decades—younger. I'll never be an Olympic swimmer, of course, but I tell myself that's because I never learned to swim, not because I'm too old. I'll never run a marathon, because I have shin splints and bad knees, not because I'm twice the age of many competing runners today. Like my friend, I think of myself as much younger than my chronological age. And it really hurts when others see only the years, and not the spirit.

Such feelings may be one of the reasons I've discovered that I like working with older people. In the first place, they are older than I am, and that's a definite plus. I get to be the kid. I get to hear such sweet reassurances as "Oh, my dear, you're so young," or "You're much too young to remember that."

In the second place, they mother me. They delight in my triumphs, laugh at my jokes, indulge me in my weaknesses, give me solace in my sadness, and reprimand me for my excesses. They think I'm cute, sweet, and wonderful. Their attention makes me feel anything is possible. It makes me feel charming. It makes me feel *young,* at least until I step back into the real world and people expect me to "act my age."

And if I am tired in my forties of acting my age, how must someone seventy, eighty, or ninety feel? Any hint of behavior outside the norm is likely to brand them "senile" or "confused." Just being elderly gets people in trouble when others attach stereotypes to their chronological age. "He's almost eighty-two, for heaven's sake—what do you expect?"

About limits and expectations

I got a call last year from the small town in Virginia where my parents live, meaning I got a call from the housekeeper who cares for my parents. My father had been making noises about going back into business. That day, he had demanded the phone book so he could contact suppliers he had dealt with when he was in business before. The housekeeper and my mother were frightened by his insistence. He might embarrass himself, they said.

When I finally talked with Dad on the phone, I found out that he was a bit confused about a building we had sold that he thought he still owned. He wanted to make some calls about fixing up the building. After we had settled the fact that the building had already been sold, I asked him whether he'd been thinking about it because he was considering going back into business.

"Well, yes," he said in the strong businessman's voice I have not heard in years. We talked about that for a while, and he agreed to wait until I came to discuss the idea further.

My father will never go back into business, but that day, I didn't see a crazy, confused eighty-year-old man. I saw a man who had been very ill for the past two years and who had been severely depressed about the uselessness of his existence. Perhaps he had opened his eyes that morning and said, "What in the world am I going to do with the rest of my life?"

For two years, he had been sitting around acting his age, doing what society dictates his age acts like. At least for one day, he had decided to act the way he felt—like a much younger man who had been good at his work and wanted something productive to do. The idea that he shouldn't or couldn't never entered his mind.

There's no real end to the story. It's a conversation I continue to have with him from time to time. And whenever I think about how he acts in those moments, I realize that at any age there are things society decides we just aren't capable of doing, because we are either too young or too old, or because it would be unseemly for us to attempt such a project. In my middle years I find myself hemmed in by such limitations more and more often. The decisions I make about things I want to accomplish, places I want to go, are increasingly colored by time. I cannot deny that I am perhaps more tuned in to do all that I want to do because of my role as caregiver and my work with frail older persons. I see their regrets. I hear their remorse at not having planned better or acted sooner. And I cannot deny that it creates in me a certain anxiety, and even panic.

And my limitations are not all in my mind. I notice physical hindrances starting to creep in on me. Periodically a bad back brings me face-to-face with the reality of disability. I had always thought that if I had a functioning mind, I could adapt to a failing body. A couple of winters ago, however, an injury put that naive philosophy to the test.

After a snowstorm, each flake held so much water that a shovelful felt like a ton. I was clearing the front walk, cursing the elements with each lift of the shovel until I felt a wrenching, tearing pull in my back. I ended up in a reclining chair with heating pads and pain killers for the next ten days. On paper ten days does not sound like a very long time, but confinement to bed makes it seem an eternity. During the long hours of those days, I thought a lot about physical incapacity, and I learned some valuable lessons.

I learned that, even though I knew that I eventually would recover, sometimes I did not feel sure. I was occasionally afraid that the pain that prevented my sitting or standing would persist for another month or even longer. I tried to be rational, but because back injuries are hard to diagnose at best, it did seem possible that some damage might be permanent.

I also learned a painful lesson in humility. For those ten days, I had to rely on someone else to do everything for me. I was so used to functioning solo that my dependency seemed ridiculous, even embarrassing. My husband had come home and helped me get settled with work, TV, reading materials, telephone, and bag lunch. I had insisted he return to work. It was a wrenched back—no big deal. I'd be up and around in no time.

About an hour later, I had to go to the bathroom. "No problem," I thought.

Major problem. It took me several minutes just to ease the chair (and my body) to an upright position. Then I had to crawl because that was the least painful way to move. I had to pull myself onto the toilet and crawl back to my chair. I was exhausted, as if I had done an hour of aerobics.

And then there was the need to ask for everything. "Please, bring me...As long as you're up, could you?" My meals were delivered on a tray. After the mail was delivered, I had to wait until my husband came home to see it. For a basically independent person to be so suddenly and so completely dependent was frustrating and humiliating; I hated it.

The other lesson I learned was about taking my physical health for granted. I'm a person who every once in a while checks in with the doctor just because it seems to be about time I did. He tells me how healthy I am, and I go on my way. I play tennis. I walk several miles at a time. And in the beginning of my convalescence, I have to admit I felt the slightest bit of pleasure about having time to read and catch up on my "soaps." My enforced inactivity seemed like a perfect opportunity to indulge myself with no guilt.

After four or five days, and then a week, when the injury was no better, I focused on one thought: when would I be free of pain? For a person who had believed that physical injury was mind over matter, my mind was definitely losing this battle.

Now I appreciated the trials of those who must spend their days in a wheelchair; who must navigate by clinging to a walker or cane and moving hesitantly one foot and then the other; of those who sometimes would rather stay home than undergo the ordeal of getting dressed. I thought about those people who have had a stroke and fought to regain any part of their former function. I thought about asking for help every time I needed to go to the bathroom, depending on someone else to cut up my food, to feed me, to puree my food because I could no longer swallow solids.

I thought of sitting while others raced to and fro, free to come and go and move at will. I knew that, in such circumstances, my emotions would be mixed—gratitude for their help, but resentment of their independence. No, my ability to fully use my mind could not completely balance any loss of my body.

After ten days, I was able to get up and move gingerly, but freely. In two weeks, I was back to normal. But I was different, more aware of my independence. Now when I am with friends in wheelchairs, I ask whether I may assist them rather than just assuming they will be grateful. I ask for advice and opinions, letting people with physical impairments know that their minds and ideas are important to me. And I try never to forget what it felt like to live with a healthy mind in an injured body.

About anxiety and the importance of finding support

One of the most difficult undercurrents in giving care to another person is the often subconscious fear that what you see is what you yourself are going to get. Particularly if you are caring for parents, it is impossible not to see their frailties and wonder whether in fact you are looking into your hereditary future. If you are caring for a spouse, will you develop infirmities simply because of the stress during these years of caring for him?

The power of such fears and their impact on caregiving cannot be underestimated. Whether or not such anxiety is acknowledged, it adds to the stress and apprehension that often accompany what may seem like routine duties. Many caregivers talk about feeling "scared" or "panic-stricken," even in situations where the tasks are not yet particularly demanding.

It is important to know that such feelings are not unusual. Even if we are not caring for ill dependents, all of us see enough pain in this world to keep us up at night worrying about our own health futures.

A long list of ailments commonly plague older people. One way you can calm some of your fears is to find out what you are up against by asking your relative's doctor for an exact diagnosis and prognosis. This knowledge is tempered by the realization that a person's health needs may change in minutes following a catastrophic event such as a fall or stroke.

Fortunately, caregivers can get information and education as well as the encouragement of professionals and peers in the *support group.* These are people with like problems who gather for the purpose of sharing information, education, and counseling. In the process of exchanging stories with one another, members of the groups share some laughs as well as some tears. But they receive more than simple moral support. Many organizations invite speakers and distribute information about issues that directly affect caregiving.

One support group in a year of monthly meetings offered its members information on legal and financial issues, instruction in basic emergency procedures, demonstrations of new products to make life easier for disabled persons, sessions on stress and time management as well as grief counseling and the opportunity to share with each other and a trained leader their own frustrations and triumphs. The first piece of advice I offer any caregiver is, join a support group. Yet most caregivers never join. Why? It's a question health care professionals have been asking themselves for years. The best answers I've heard have come from caregivers themselves. See if you can see yourself in any of the following statements:

OBJECTION: I don't have time to breathe now—how in the world can I make time for a meeting?

ANSWER: You'd best find time. The benefits you receive in a support group can ease your work and help you be more efficient, assist you in finding more time, and enable you to give care over the long term without burning out.

OBJECTION: I don't need to hear other people's sad stories—I have enough grief of my own.

ANSWER: Yes, you do need to hear the stories of others in order to understand that you are not alone. You need the benefit of sharing their experience and your own, and the knowledge that you have supported others whose circumstances resemble yours.

OBJECTION: Is that like AA?

ANSWER: We are not talking about a dependency here, although in some cases caregivers do function as codependents, taking over the relative's life and not allowing her to function even to her limited capacity.

OBJECTION: I work.

ANSWER: In most locations meetings are scheduled to suit the group's needs. Chances are that where you work there are other caregivers. If so, perhaps you could start a group right there. Or at your church or synagogue.

OBJECTION: I have no time to spend with my husband and children now because I'm using so much time caring for my mother.

ANSWER: Meetings are usually once a month for about an hour and a half. Take your spouse and children (if they are old enough) with you; they will gain something too in opportunities to speak out and to find ways for you as a family to limit the inroads that giving care may make into your own family life.

OBJECTION: I don't think there are any groups in my area.

ANSWER: Make some calls. Check with the hospital social services department, the office on aging in your community or county, the senior center, the local branch of such charitable groups as the Alzheimer's and Related Disorders Association, the American Diabetes Association, the American Heart Association, etc.

(For more information on support groups, see pp. 80-81.)

EXERCISES IN COPING

KNOWING THE FACTS

Caring for aging family members will become more prevalent in our society during this decade and the coming century. America is aging, and we are living longer lives. Many of us are also living healthier, more productive lives. But always some segment of the population will need care. If your family includes one or more of those persons, you will face hard choices about your own lifestyle as you make room for their care.

Fortunately, the network of support groups, literature, and other media is growing. Check with your local library or contact the agencies named below to answer questions and make your life as a caregiver easier and more rewarding.

"How can I learn about aging—what is normal; what is not?"

• Readings:

Look in the card catalog of your library under Aging; Geriatrics; Health; Medicine—Geriatrics. (If there is a university or college library nearby, use that one.)

Look in the *Reader's Guide to Periodic Literature* under the same headings for recent magazine articles on the subject.

If necessary, ask your librarian for assistance in finding the information you need.

• For more information, contact:

Your local office on aging, or clinics or hospitals with programs specializing in geriatrics.

"The person I care for has been diagnosed with . . ."

• Readings:

Check your library's card catalog under the appropriate headings: Alzheimer's disease, arthritis, diabetes, heart disease, Parkinson's disease, or stroke. If there is a medical library in your area, their information will probably be more extensive than that of a local library.

Ask your relative's physician for any literature available on your relative's condition.

- For more information:

Contact the local chapter of the national organization related to your relative's impairment or illness, such as Alzheimer's and Related Disorders Association, American Diabetes Association, or American Heart Association.

Ask your relative's physician or hospital social worker for additional sources of information.

"I'm new at this caregiving thing, but there's no doubt I'm doing more and more for my family member."

- Readings:

Check your local library for books listed under "Caregiving," "Eldercare," "Family Relationships," "Aging," or ask your librarian for help.

AARP also has a number of free and excellent materials for caregivers. Write them at AARP, 1909 K Street NW, Washington, DC 20005.

- For more information:

Join a support group where you will receive information and education as well as emotional support on an ongoing basis.

"Things are going along fine right now, but is there something I can do to get ready?"

- Readings:

If your relative has been diagnosed with any specific chronic condition (perhaps even more than one), keep current on the literature about that condition. Refer to your local library for information and seek information from your relative's physician about the prognosis for this condition and how it might affect your relative's life.

- For more information:

Start to gather information about community services and resources as early as possible. Many of the services may never be necessary, but how nice to know how to contact them if they become necessary.

"A support group might be a good idea—whom do I call?"

- For more information:

Contact the local chapter of the national organization related to your relative's condition; your local hospital social services department; the office on aging in your community; senior centers or other agencies who regularly provide support and informational services to older persons and their families.

"My relative is basically healthy but is depressed about the prospect of old age and potential frailty."

- Readings:

Unfortunately there is not a lot of material at this writing about depression in the later years. Check with your local librarian or bookstore owner for recommendations, and look at the tables of contents of recent books on depression which might possibly have a chapter about depression in older persons.

The following national organizations offer a great deal of free literature to members. Dues are nominal and well worth the opportunity to keep up with what these advocacy groups are doing to make certain your old age is a good one.

The American Association of Retired Persons (AARP), 1909 K Street NW, Washington, DC 20049.

Gray Panthers, 3700 Chestnut Street, Philadelphia, PA 10904.

National Council on Aging (NCOA), 600 Maryland Avenue SW, Washington, DC 20024.

Older Women's League (OWL), 730 11th Street NW, Washington, DC 20001.

Chapter 4

But Doesn't Medicare Pay for That?

Your ability to orchestrate your relative's care depends upon your understanding of the nitty-gritty complexities of health care in our modern society. These include the policies of bureaucratic agencies which make decisions based upon generalizations, not upon your particular situation. You also need to grasp your relative's complicated economic arrangements, including insurance, assets, debts, and other details. The information and checklists in this chapter will help you get a handle on your relative's affairs, preferably before the need for action arises. Although Medicare does an excellent job of covering treatment of acute catastrophic illness, it rarely pays the expenses of chronic, long-term care. Acute care addresses immediate, relatively urgent needs. Your mother falls, fractures a hip, is taken to the emergency room by ambulance, admitted to the hospital; she undergoes surgery, has some physical therapy, and is discharged. To this point, Medicare does a good job of covering the costs.

But what about afterwards? What about the fact that her recovery is not sufficient to allow her the full range of activities she enjoyed before the fall? What if she can no longer drive? Such an important loss has a crippling effect on her life—if she can no longer drive, she can no longer go anywhere on her own—to the store to buy groceries, to the doctor for regular check-ups, to social activities. Her disability limits her, makes her dependent on others, and, to some extent, isolates her.

The demographic portrait of an older person in America depicts a white female, widowed, living on limited income with one or more chronic disabilities that restrict ability to function independently.

In limited cases *under current rules,* Medicare covers some home care. If your mother is unable to get out for physical therapy, for example, the physician may write an order for a therapist to come to her home for a limited period. More basic home help, such as an aide's assistance with household chores and personal care such as bathing, is tied to the provision of a professional service. In other words, if your mother has no need for the professional services of either an R.N. or certified therapist at home, she is not eligible for coverage of an aide or chore service.

Such "Catch-22" rules often catch caregivers unawares. Unfortunately many a caregiver is surprised when the hospital discharges her father before he is ready to resume life in the community. She often expects that Medicare covers all costs of care up to and including nursing home expenses, but she soon finds that these expectations are too optimistic.

UNDERSTANDING THE HEALTH CARE LINGO

To innocent ears, Medicare and insurance jargon sounds like a foreign language. Caregivers need some basic knowledge of financial terminology and legalities. To complicate matters, the rules, which are subject to administrative and budgetary changes, are unstable. Local policies may differ from state to state. Caregivers must stay abreast of current circumstances, which may alter after the publication of this book.

DRG

This is a term you may hear bandied about while your relative is in the hospital. The abbreviation stands for "diagnostic-related groups" and means that the federal government has set some time limits on hospital stays based on what it estimates is a reasonable stay for a certain condition. Someone who has suffered a hip fracture falls into one of these DRGs. For the hospital to be reimbursed by Medicare for services provided to patients, it must abide by DRGs as closely as possible. And that fact sets in motion a series of issues related to medical cost.

Medicare

This health insurance program, funded and administered by the federal government, is for people sixty-five and older and for some disabled persons. Medicare covers 80 percent of *accepted* charges for acute care in hospitals, clinics, and doctors' offices. But coverage isn't nearly as simple as that statement sounds.

In the first place, there are two parts to Medicare. Part A serves as hospital insurance and covers inpatient hospital stays, some inpatient *skilled* nursing home care, some home health care services, and some hospice care. Part B is a medical insurance which covers *medically necessary* doctors' services, some therapies, some outpatient services, and some medical equipment.

According to its mandate under the Social Security Act MEDICARE COVERS ONLY CARE WHICH IT DEEMS REASONABLE AND NECESSARY. (The translation of this statement is that Medicare is not set up to cover preventive medical care.) Nor does it cover what it deems to be "custodial" or maintenance care. In short, there must be a medical need for services, which thus must result in progress toward wellness.

Obviously, there are certain services and situations NOT covered under either Part A or B. These include an assortment of needs:

Items and services not directly related to the diagnosis and treatment of a specific illness or injury
Health care outside the United States
Personal comfort or convenience items
Routine physical check-ups
Eyeglasses or examinations except as related to cataracts
Hearing examinations or aids

Routine foot care except as related directly to an illness such as diabetes
Dental services
Custodial care, which is generally provided by unskilled personnel
Home-delivered meals
Domestic or housekeeping services
Transportation services, except for covered ambulance services
Items or services which are covered under another insurer, such as automobile insurance or employer insurance.

Both Parts A and B have deductible amounts that you pay out-of-pocket or through another insurance before Medicare starts to pay. Part A covers the first sixty days of a hospital stay, including semi-private room, nursing services, supplies and equipment, and other such expenses, after payment of the deductible ($628 in 1991). After that the insured is responsible for partial payment. Part A also pays for some home care, some *skilled* care in nursing homes, and some hospice care.

Part B is a voluntary insurance program that carries a monthly premium which is automatically deducted from the person's Social Security check each month. There is also an additional $100 annual deductible. Part B pays only 80 percent of "assigned" fees (see below), including physician services, diagnostic tests and x-rays, some prosthetic devices such as pacemakers and colostomy bags, and some outpatient services.

The Medicare subscriber receives a Medicare card showing a claim number, the date coverage began, and whether the coverage includes Parts A and B.

One more trick of the trade: find out whether the physician or institution "accepts assignment." Again the government has assigned the fees which it deems acceptable for various services. Medicare has established, for example, the maximum amount which it pays for an office visit or x-ray. If the physician "accepts assignment," it means that she thereby agrees to charge no more than the federally established fee for service. If the physician does NOT accept assignment, then you pay the difference between the "assigned" amount and the doctor's actual charges. In most communities a listing of physicians who accept assignment is available. Call the local medical society or office on aging.

There is some good news: As of September 1990, ALL doctors are required by federal law to submit claims to Medicare for their Medicare patients. (In the past a physician had the option of filing the claim or leaving that job to the patient.) The new law requires all doctors—whether or not they accept assignment—to file all claims for Medicare, AND they are prohibited from charging for this service.

After the claim has been filed and acted on by Medicare, your relative receives a paper that looks like the one on pages 50 and 51. This is your explanation of a particular Medicare benefit. Note that it includes the following information:

1. Name of insurer—the "carrier" or "intermediary," which means the company that handles the claim for the government. If you receive medical care in different states, the "carrier" varies. This entry includes the phone number to contact for questions.
2. Name and address of the patient.
3. Health insurance claim number (the patient's Social Security number plus a letter).
4. Notice of assignment whether accepted or not; claim number; amount of claim and name of service provider.
5. Service, date of service, amount billed, amount approved.
6. Remarks.
7. Total approved amount, 80 percent of approved amount, and recipient (patient or physician or applied to deductible).
8. Explanation of remarks.
9. Notice of deductible.
10. Notice of process for appealing this notice.

The patient receives this document every time services are submitted for payment. As it clearly states, it is NOT a bill, but rather an explanation of benefits. It is ALSO an important document to file for supplemental coverage from a private carrier.

Supplemental insurance

A number of private companies offer health insurance that pays all or part of the services Medicare does not cover and the 20 percent which it does not

Mailing Address
MEDICARE

YOUR EXPLANATION OF MEDICARE BENEFITS

Please Read This Notice Carefully And Keep It For Your Records

THIS IS NOT A BILL

HEALTHCARE FINANCING ADMINISTRATION

02/20/91 PAGE: 01 015089

① NEED HELP? CONTACT:

③ YOUR HEALTH INSURANCE CLAIM NUMBER

FOR MEDICAL SERVICES YOU RECEIVE ON OR AFTER SEPTEMBER 1, 1990, YOUR DOCTOR OR THE COMPANY THAT PROVIDES YOUR MEDICAL SERVICES, EQUIPMENT OR SUPPLIES MUST PREPARE AND SUBMIT YOUR PART B MEDICARE CLAIMS.

PARTICIPATING DOCTORS AND SUPPLIERS ALWAYS ACCEPT ASSIGNMENT OF MEDICARE CLAIMS.SEE THE BACK OF THIS NOTICE FOR AN EXPLANATION OF ASSIGNMENT. WRITE OR CALL US FOR THE NAME OF A PARTICIPATING DOCTOR OR SUPPLIER OR FOR A FREE LIST OF PARTICIPATING DOCTORS AND SUPPLIERS.

④ YOUR DOCTOR OR SUPPLIER DID NOT ACCEPT ASSIGNMENT OF YOUR CLAIM (CONTROL NO. 91035-0121900) FOR $ 21.80. (SEE ITEM 4 ON BACK).

⑤ DR	PROCEDURE		BILLED	APPROVED
1	OFFICE SERVICE(S) 90040	JAN 29-JAN 29,1991	$ 21.80	$ 16.80

APPROVED AMOUNT LIMITED BY ITEM 5C ON BACK.

⑥ REMARK CODES: A O

⑦ NO PAYMENT IS BEING MADE TO YOU BECAUSE THE TOTAL APPROVED AMOUNT OF $ 16.80 WAS APPLIED TOWARD YOU ANNUAL DEDUCTIBLE.

IF YOU HAVE OTHER INSURANCE, IT MAY HELP WITH THE PART MEDICARE DID NOT PAY.

⑧ EXPLANATION OF REMARK CODES:
A- NEXT TIME YOU REQUEST PAYMENT, USE YOUR MEDICARE CLAIM NUMBER AS IT IS SHOWN ON THIS NOTICE.
O-

GI-56733 REV. 4-89 PRINTED IN U.S.A.

Mailing Address
MEDICARE

YOUR EXPLANATION OF MEDICARE BENEFITS

Please Read This Notice Carefully And Keep It For Your Records

THIS IS NOT A BILL

HEALTHCARE FINANCING ADMINISTRATION

02/20/91 PAGE: 02 015090

NEED HELP? CONTACT:

YOUR HEALTH INSURANCE CLAIM NUMBER

⑨ YOU HAVE NOW MET $ 16.80 OF THE $100.00 DEDUCTIBLE FOR 1991.

⑩ IMPORTANT IF YOU DO NOT AGREE WITH THE AMOUNTS APPROVED YOU MAY ASK FOR A REVIEW. TO DO THIS YOU MUST WRITE TO US BEFORE AUG 20, 1991 (SEE ITEM 1 ON THE BACK).

DO YOU HAVE ANY QUESTIONS ABOUT THIS NOTICE? IF YOU BELIEVE MEDICARE PAID FOR A SERVICE YOU DID NOT RECEIVE, OR THERE IS AN ERROR, CONTACT US IMMEDIATELY. ALWAYS GIVE US THE:

MEDICARE CLAIM NO. CLAIM CONTROL NO. FOR CLAIM IN QUESTION.

GI-56733 REV. 4-89 PRINTED IN U.S.A.

pay even for the services it does cover. This kind of policy is called supplemental or "Medigap" insurance. Policies and state regulations vary; you may have to apply for these payments yourself if your physician or clinic does not submit the claim for you. (The new law requires only that they submit for Medicare payment, not supplemental insurance.)

When purchasing a supplemental policy, compare several policies. Seek the advice of others who currently have a supplemental policy and of local advocates for older persons in your area.

Medicaid or Title XIX

For people with very low incomes, every state has some form of the Medicaid program that covers some items which Medicare does not allow. Eligibility requirements and coverage vary from state to state. Medicaid is a state-operated, federally funded program. A recipient must meet several eligibility requirements:

- Sixty-five years or older, blind, disabled, or a parent with a dependent child
- U.S. citizen or legal alien
- Resident of the state in which he is applying for aid
- Financially needy, with an income below established limits.

Home health care

In response to the idea that people generally do better in their own homes and communities than in institutions, alternative options are developing. The home care industry has arisen to answer the need for community care. Medicare covers some of the home care services which are vital in this day of limited hospital stays and early discharges:

- Part-time nursing care supervised by a registered nurse
- Physical, speech, or occupational therapy administered by a trained professional

- Social services and counseling administered by a trained social worker under the direction of a physician

- Medical supplies and appliances necessary for the home care or treatment of an illness or injury

- Limited services of a home health aide as one part of a total care plan that includes the services of a skilled professional such as a nurse or therapist

Medicare will NOT cover the following homecare services:

- Health aides who are not working as part of a plan that includes professional or skilled services

- Self-administered medications

- Home-delivered meals

- Housekeeping or chore services

- Transportation

Medicare pays home care benefits only in specific circumstances:

- The agency is Medicare-certified (an important question to ask when selecting an agency).

- The agency files a claim.

- The physician certifies the need for prescribed care.

- A care plan is established.

- The patient is "homebound" or confined to home (unable to leave without major assistance or use of a wheelchair, walker, or other ambulatory device).

- The patient needs *skilled* care on at least an intermittent basis.

The word "skilled" comes into any discussion about Medicare coverage of home care. You need to understand that a skilled professional (nurse, physician, or therapist) needn't administer the care directly; it can be given by a lay worker supervised by such a professional.

At the time of this writing, nothing in the Medicare mandate covering home care distinguishes chronic from acute illness. Unfortunately, however, a sort of unwritten interpretation has developed that home care benefits should stop when patients are no longer acutely ill. According to the Center for Public Representation in Madison, Wisconsin, that interpretation by Medicare intermediaries has "no basis in law and should be appealed."[1]

One of the terms you may hear as you work with an aging relative is "spending down." In more sophisticated circles, the term "divestment" may crop up. What everyone is talking about is the exhaustion of assets while the person remains in the community, before he needs to move to a nursing home.

Some people transfer their money, their homes, and other assets either as gifts or at a minimal price, to a family member so that the asset is no longer in the name of the potential Medicaid applicant.

Most states will deny Title XIX eligibility to any person residing in a nursing home who has transferred any asset for less than its fair market value shortly before applying for Medicaid. The length of denial depends upon the value of the asset and the state's decision. If you have questions, contact your state's office on aging and ask for an interpretation BEFORE you make decisions about disposal of assets.

In the past, spouses who remained in the community were often reduced to poverty when patients entered nursing homes. This problem became such a scandal that the law now allows a spouse to keep her home and its contents, a car, and, in some states, one half (up to $60,000) of the couple's assets for as long as that person occupies the home. (Check with your state office on aging for specifics in your state.)

[1]Center for Public Representation *Your Real Medicare Handbook,* Madison, Wis., 1989, p. 25.

UNDERSTANDING THE LEGAL LINGO

Some legal matters need attention in case the person you are caring for becomes physically or mentally incapacitated:

Durable power of attorney

Contact your relative's lawyer as early as possible in the caregiving process to learn about power of attorney and durable power of attorney in your relative's state. In some places, they are the same, but in other situations, simple power of attorney dissolves if a person becomes incapacitated—the time when you and your relative are most likely to need it. The *durable* power of attorney continues in spite of incapacity. There also may be a difference between a POA for financial decisions and one for health-related decisions. Check your state law.

As soon as possible you need to encourage your older relatives to name a representative and sign the papers necessary to make the appointment legal. Explain that such an appointment need not go into effect unless some incapacity occurs; this action allows a person to retain control over her life via a spokesman she has chosen herself.

Guardianship

If a relative has become too mentally incapacitated to appoint a POA, you may need to set up a guardianship. This process varies from state to state. Your attorney can advise you on the particulars.

Joint tenancy

This legal arrangement protects your relative's property, including real estate, bank accounts, stocks, bonds, and other assets, if he becomes incapacitated. It allows co-ownership and management of property. The kicker is that neither party can dispose of the property without the consent of the other, which is where the protection comes in. In some states, ownership of property held in joint tenancy reverts to the co-owner at the death of the partner. As a caregiver, you need to learn the advantages and disadvantages of this and the other legal safeguards discussed here before you make any decisions.

Living will

An increasing number of states have passed legislation allowing persons to state their wishes about "heroic measures" during life-threatening illness. These "right-to-die" legal documents assist a family and medical community to make decisions which are guided by knowledge of a patient's preferences. Sometimes challenges to the decision arise, even when such a document exists. If your state has not passed a living-will law, it is nevertheless wise to talk with your family about the issue so that all of you can be reassured by making your feelings known. Some people say, "I don't want to be hooked up to any machines." Others decide, "I want to be kept alive by every means possible in case a miracle happens."

EXERCISES IN COPING

GETTING ORGANIZED

Americans characteristically deny aging as well as death. In the flush of our youth and even our middle-age we make blanket statements. "If I ever get Alzheimer's, . . ." we say. "If I'm ever in a wheelchair. . . ." Even so, we lack conviction that such an outcome might be possible for us. Those sorts of things happen to others—not ME. Even in our middle years, we see ourselves as invincible. Madison Avenue has told us that if we buy enough of the right product, if we join the right club, play the right sport, eat the right food, wear the accepted labels, take the magic pills, we can resist nature.

But being prepared is a major factor in successfully coping with care of aging relatives as well as with aging itself: prepared for incapacity, for catastrophic events, for making decisions about issues of health and property.

Here are some basic facts that will help you deal with the ins and outs of the financial and legal system for long-term care:

1. Understand the lingo. What is a DRG? What are Medicare and Medicaid or Title XIX? What services are included under home health care and how do you qualify for them? What is divestment of assets? Spousal impoverishment? If you are an adult child caring for a parent or in-law, do you have any legal or financial responsibility? What is supplemental insurance? A living will? What are "heroic measures"?

2. Get the financial facts. What are your relative's current assets, her income? Where are the important papers, such as deeds, wills, insurance policies, bank books? Who is her financial advisor? Who has power of attorney? Is that power "durable"? Is there a necessity for guardianship or joint tenancy? Has she written a living will? Is there, indeed, a will of any kind?

3. Work with your health team. What is the physician willing to order for home health care following a hospitalization? What services can the social worker or discharge planner suggest? What programs are available in the community to help both you and your relative return to a "normal" lifestyle?

4. Be prepared. Talk to your relative before a catastrophe occurs to learn his ideas and wishes in the event of an illness or the need for chronic care. Investigate options with your relative and try to involve him as much as possible in decisions.

5. Get started as early as you can. Talking about such things as wills and power of attorney even when you are well and middle-aged causes stress. After a major stroke or surgery, this discussion alarms people. Try to settle at least the basic issues as soon as possible:

- Appoint a durable power of attorney.
- Establish the location of all important documents: Medicare card, birth certificate, will, insurance policies, and other legal papers.
- Establish your relative's wishes about care during either mental or physical incapacity.
- Set up a file system to record otherwise confusing reimbursement for Medicare and supplemental insurance coverage that may be paid directly to the patient.

- Make sure he has a will.
- Establish exact assets, including pensions and veterans' benefits, and locate the papers which document those assets.
- Establish relationships with an attorney, senior citizen advocacy group, office-on-aging representative, or financial planner.

Complete the following checklist for your relative:

Name of Person: ______________________________

Address: ______________________________

Social Security Number: ______________________________

Medicare Number: ______________________________

PROFESSIONAL NAME	ADDRESS	PHONE
Physician		
HMO dentist		
Attorney		
Insurance agent		

Financial planner

Clergyperson

DOCUMENT	LOCATION	IDENTITY NUMBER
Birth certificate		
Bank statements		
Citizenship papers		
Deed(s)		
Divorce decrees		
Insurance policies		
Life		
Health		
Supplemental		
Auto		
Homeowner's		
Leases		
Marriage certificate		

DOCUMENT	LOCATION	IDENTITY NUMBER
Medical records		
Medicare files		
Medicare card		
Military records		
Mortgages		
Income tax returns		
Passports		
Power of attorney		
Savings account passbooks		
Receipts		
Social Security card		
Stock certificates		
Titles		

DOCUMENT	LOCATION	IDENTITY NUMBER
Warranties		
Wills		

INVESTMENTS (enter total value of each)	LOCATION
Cash in checking, savings, etc.	
Certificates of deposit	
Trusts	
Mutual funds/money market funds	
Stocks (list)	
Bonds	
Real estate	
Interest in business	

CREDIT CARDS	NUMBER

INSURANCE TYPE	POLICY NUMBER	PREMIUM	DATE DUE
Life			
Health			
Supplemental			
Auto			
Homeowner's			
Other			

MEDICATIONS	STRENGTH	DOSAGE	PRESCRIBING PHYSICIAN

ALLERGIES AND OTHER DRUG REACTIONS

ASSETS

Cash on hand

Checking accounts

Savings accounts

Credit union account

Other savings (CDs, IRAs, Keoghs)

House (market value)

Other real estate

Household furnishings

Automobiles (Blue Book value)

Life insurance (cash value)

Stocks (current market)

Profit sharing

Bonds

Money owed to person

Personal property (jewelry, collections, etc.)

Other

LIABILITIES

Mortgages (balance)

Loans

Installment debts

Credit cards

Insurance premiums

Taxes

Other bills

Other debts

All of these financial and legal matters need your attention as early in the caregiving process as possible; some situations require attention before care begins. Maintaining control for and with your relative and knowing the whole picture of her financial and legal situation are vital elements in your ability to cope over the long haul. If your relative is unwilling to confide in you or disclose information, enlist the aid of a trusted advisor or friend.

Chapter 5

History Lessons and Attitude Adjustments

Sometimes in the afternoons at the daycare center where I work, we play music while we help clients bundle up against the elements for the ride home. It's usually a recording of Lawrence Welk or Mitch Miller. Sometimes someone starts to whistle or sing along. Staff members occasionally do an impromptu dance step as they move among clients helping with buttons and mittens that must go over fingers that no longer work. Some of the songs the staff knows; some only the clients recognize.

During this routine the other day, I wondered how things will be when I'm eighty and attending a daycare center. Will they play Barbra Streisand, Neil Diamond, or Peter, Paul and Mary? Will the staff know about the Kingston Trio and Poor Charlie on the MTA (did he ever return)? Will I sing again the songs of my youth, "Blowin' in the Wind" or "If I Had a Hammer"? Will the Beatles play on?

Understanding history is another form of taking a walk in our clients' shoes. It builds understanding and communication. It strengthens relationships and helps us cope with the frustrations of caring for people whose health is inevitably declining.

The 1987 stock market crash released a flood of memories for people who had lived through far more devastating losses in 1929. Although our clients told some stories of those depression years with sadness and even tears, they nevertheless remembered that time with pride. "We survived," their faces seemed to say. And we younger people felt a new respect for the spirit of folks in their late eighties or older, who were then in their twenties and thirties, scared and struggling. These people know what it is to survive hard times; we can only imagine. They made it; if it happens again, maybe we can too.

Of course, we older and younger people also share some history. Where were you when Kennedy was shot? I remember. So do they. And fashion—try talking to a woman in her eighties about the shock of seeing short skirts in the twenties or pants when Katherine Hepburn began wearing them in public. Compare today's world with life when our elders were young. They have interesting things to say about war and peace, morals, elections, the World Series, and every other imaginable subject. For his eightieth birthday, my sister gave Dad a beginning collection of baseball cards, including some real old-timers. As he flipped through the cards, I was astounded by his knowledge. He knew the players, their positions, their teams—we're talking about baseball from fifty or sixty years ago, and not only about players everyone knows, like Babe Ruth.

I knew Dad had been a baseball fan in his youth—he had played third base on a local team, but I never realized how much he knew or how much he enjoyed the game. My sister knew, as did her husband. Over the years, he and Dad had spent the occasional Saturday watching baseball and other sports on TV.

Later, when we watched a couple of Series games together, I was struck by his perceptive commentary. The man knows baseball. That side of him was new to me, unexplored, exciting when I had thought I knew him so well.

When I returned to work, I looked at those old faces differently. I led discussions and asked for others' opinions instead of offering mine. The pleasure on the face of a person who is seventy-plus when someone asks for his opinion is an experience not to be missed.

Think about it. In a world where they are mostly being told what to do, and talked *about* rather than *with* by well-meaning professionals, relatives, and others, when somebody actually asks what they think, it is an event. When a frail person's body is crippled by stroke, arthritis, diabetes, or cancer, it's easy to assume that her mind is crippled as well, and that she needs help with everything, even thinking. But even people with mental impairments and limitations have opinions. The Alzheimer's patient may exist only in the moment, but in that moment he thinks thoughts.

The stressful, immediate demands of giving care crowd our days. We want to know our clients or relatives personally, but we put that concern on the back burner. In fact it may never show up on the stove at all. "I know her," you protest. "She's my mother—I've known her all my life."

Maybe. But probably not. In any relationship, even the closest ones, there are surprises. They may be the spice that keeps life interesting. No matter how well we think we know our spouse or best friend or sibling or parent, they invariably do or say something that takes us by surprise. "I never knew you felt that way," we say, feeling sheepish about the unexplored chasm between us.

Fortunately it is never too late to know another person, and getting to know your dependent makes your job immeasurably easier. I especially try to remember that when I meet an older person who seems mad at the whole world. Edna was such a person. She criticized and glared at everything around her. She refused to participate in any activity. She rejected every suggestion or idea. I had two choices: I could accept at face value the persona Edna presented, or I could wonder, What's going on here? I normally choose the latter option, because it's more interesting, and it's more productive.

Edna, it turned out, was indeed angry. She was also depressed and lonely and shy and very vulnerable. She was angry because, at a time in her life when she had expected to be enjoying her husband's companionship, he had died. So had a number of her friends. Other friends whose husbands were still living had slowly drifted away. Edna had never driven a car, so she was bound to the house in the suburbs where she and her husband had raised their three children. When she wasn't watching younger neighbors hurry off to work, to social gatherings and meetings, she was waiting for her own children and grandchildren to visit or take her to the store or to church.

Although she had always been proud and meticulous, now Edna began to neglect her appearance, her nutrition, her health. Alone in the large house with only her dog and the TV for company, she began to lose track of time. What was the point? she decided; no one cared. One day was pretty much the same as the next.

Alarmed, her children made their move. They took her to a doctor who admitted her to the hospital for evaluation. Her children signed her up for daycare. They took turns having her stay with them in their houses. They took over all her decision making.

By the time I met her at the daycare center, she was understandably frustrated. On the one hand, she had gotten some of what she wanted—attention and concern from her family, some relief from full responsibility for her life, a more interesting daily routine. But at what cost?

Gradually Edna's charming, wry sense of humor resurfaced in our conversations. This lady was funny—she looked at the world around her and saw the humor and the irony of it. And as we shared a laugh now and then, we shared other things as well. And, she opened up more with her family. They were delighted to have back the witty Mom who had raised them.

Edna was capable of resuming command of much of her life. People who are not capable of major decision making also need understanding of their thoughts about the world and assistance to adapt to the changes frailty and old age have foisted upon them. I work with some ladies in a Tuesday craft group. Some members of my group have Alzheimer's disease; others have suffered strokes. Complicating their primary diagnosis are impairments such as aphasia (loss of ability to talk), arthritis, paralysis, diabetes, mild confusion, depression. Such a diverse group is a challenge to plan for, since what I think one may be able to do, two others may not be able to manage at all. Each Tuesday is an experiment.

One member of the group is Sara, a small, wiry woman, slightly intimidating, who gets about in her wheelchair. As a result of her stroke, she does not speak—at least not with her voice. Her eyes and facial expressions, on the other hand, speak volumes. She clearly is a bright and independent soul who suffers the rage and depression that often accompany a debilitating event such as a stroke. She cannot move any body part on the left side. Her inability to speak falsely suggests that she is somehow mentally impaired as well.

Like Edna, Sara probably comes to the daycare center more out of an agreement with her family than because she wants to be there. I watch her reaction as a measure of the interest and challenge of the program. She doesn't have much patience with some of our foolishness, and she has found a way to speak loudly and clearly when a program does not live up to her standards. She vigorously wheels herself with one hand up the aisle and toward the door.

I have a lot of respect for Sara. I think she knows that. Slowly during the several weeks since she joined my craft group, we have come to a mutual understanding of what each of us is about. At first I saw the distrust in her eyes as I started to lay out a simple project for the group. She had been patronized before, and she didn't intend to tolerate further condescension.

Older people are more accepting of a project, no matter how simple it may be, if it has a purpose. If it's more than "busy work," people tend to relax and get more involved. They also appreciate choices and opportunities for decisions. Again, the words, "What do you think?" can work miracles.

As the weeks went by, and Sara began to trust that what we were doing had some purpose, she began to relax. I saw her body loosen and her facial tension let go. Instead, she began to concentrate intensely as she tried to do the work. She also began to consider the rest of the group, watching my interactions with them, understanding and accepting their disabilities and frailties, rejoicing with them in small victories of accomplishment.

In December, we completed a simple Christmas ornament that I would have spent about five minutes making. The job had cost each member of the group a full hour. At the end of the session, Sara looked at me and smiled; it was a slight lifting of the corner of her mouth, but unmistakably a smile. Even though I had, at her request, done most of the work for her, she had made the choices.

A week later when I invited her to the group, she immediately released the wheelchair brake, indicating her permission for me to steer her to the table. Our project that day was more difficult, pinning fabric squares to a styrofoam form. Painstakingly, Sara clinched a pin in her mouth as she placed the fabric just so. Then she speared the fabric with the pin. Once the first pin was in, I showed her how to take a second pin, catching the fabric and bunching it to give a more textured effect. She nodded and repeated the action.

Sara spent an entire hour with frequent rest stops, attaching one short row of fabric. But she did it herself, with only occasional help from me, and when we were done for the day, she flexed her cramped fingers and collapsed back against her wheelchair. Although she was clearly exhausted by the intensity of her efforts, she exhibited none of her usual tension.

"Good work, Sara," I said as I placed her project on the storage cart ready for the next session. I half expected to hear her customary growl. Sara eloquently dismisses anything she feels is patronizing—she simply waves one hand, looks away, and growls with disgust.

This time, Sara did not growl. She looked at her work and then at me and nodded. Her eyes said with pride, "It is good work, isn't it?" And when I massaged her hand and told her with mock seriousness that she'd better work out with those fingers every day so she'd be ready for next week, she ducked her head shyly and giggled.

Speaking of wheelchairs, during my years of working with older people, they have raised my consciousness on several fronts. One of my most important strides was acquiring an understanding of what it means to live with a quad cane, a walker, or a wheelchair as a constant companion.

I used to say that people who used wheelchairs were "confined" to that vehicle. Someone remarked that such negative language reinforces stereotypes about disability. I began to pay closer attention to the fact that the help of walkers, canes, chairs enables their users to remain mobile and independent.

These people come in all sorts of personality packages, and their attitudes about using such devices are equally varied. There's Harriet, a feisty woman of over ninety years who wheels around as freely as most people walk. She puts her wheelchair to work for her, traveling from the society of her friends to the smoking area where she enjoys one of her three-a-day cigarettes, to the dining room for lunch, to an exercise session or craft class. "Excuse me," I've heard her announce to her friends, "but I hear the music for exercises and I don't want to be late." And off she goes.

Peter has a similar attitude about his wheelchair. It is simply a device that allows him mobility, and for that he is grateful. I might not have expected that of him, for here is a man clearly accustomed to his personal freedom. He has walked across most of Europe, camped in the wilds of Canada, shot the rapids of the Grand Canyon, all after he was past seventy, and he hoboed around the country as a young man during the Great Depression. He is a bright, inquisitive, adventurous man, and one of the most independent people I have ever met.

Finding out that he would have to spend the rest of his days in a wheelchair might have come as a terrible blow, cause for depression and anger. But Peter took the facts in stride, perhaps in the same way he has accepted much of his life. For him, as for Harriet, it is the chair that is confined, to their wishes and needs, not the other way around.

Others seem to take the cane, walker, and especially the wheelchair as symbols of their frailty and dependency. Sometimes the physician has ordered daily walks, but some of these people fight the exercise, preferring to remain in their chairs. One lady used to bring her walker every day to the daycare center she attended, but once seated, she refused to stand again. "Why bring the walker?" the staff asked her. "Because my family thinks I'm using it," she replied.

Sometimes fear plays a role, especially when a bad fall resulted in the need for the supportive device in the first place. And sometimes use of an appliance just seems like too much effort. One woman with crippling arthritis used to situate herself in her favorite chair every morning and then refuse to move for the rest of the day. Asked why she didn't make use of her walker, she said, "Because I am in constant pain." Someone noted that since she was in constant pain with or without the walker, moving or sitting, she had a choice: she could either be in pain and totally confined or be in pain and use the walker to move around. Presented with that logic, she began to experiment more with the walker; eventually she was able to move throughout her home from morning to night.

Walkers in general are a pain in the neck, in some ways even more bothersome than a wheelchair. You have to find a place to stash the thing. And you have to develop a special sort of coordination in order to use it properly in the first place. Using a walker is an acquired skill that takes concentration and practice. Still, given the choice, many older people adapt. They exchange the inconvenience of their walker for the freedom to make their own breakfast rather than depend on someone to bring it to them. They use their wheelchair to get around in the community. One lady goes to and from her appointments in her wheelchair; having arrived, she moves around with her walker.

Are they confined to their wheelchairs, or are they living with them? The choice is clearly theirs. Many people live quite comfortably with their aluminum appendages, decorating them with colorful bags and carryalls, making the devices work for them. Certainly the walker or chair is not their favorite possession, but it is a fact of their life if they wish to maintain independence and maximum mobility. The attitude they take is frequently tied to their personal history, how they have handled crises and hardship in the past.

Summing Up

Working with people who range in age from fifty to more than ninety years means dealing with a lot of history, past and present. Some of it is personally familiar to me, some not. Some of it is framed in the context of history books for me and real life for them. In some cases, I can only observe something they are in fact living. Often I can only imagine their daily reality.

For some of these people, the trenches of World War I are as real as the volatile sixties are to me. At any given time, we have in the same room people who were children, others who were teen-agers, some who were grown and married, and a few who were already retired when a historical event occurred. Younger people can only speculate about how it feels to have lived for seventy or eighty years.

I think about such things as I age, watching older people, and trying hard to understand. I've learned that when I share my own frustrations or doubts or irritations about life with them, they have thoughts and understanding, and sometimes even answers for me. Working with the aged every day as I do naturally increases my empathy. My exposure is greater, my experience broader than that of most people.

I hope that, when I am eighty, someone will understand that, if I'm crabby and negative, I have a reason. And if I am critical of others, it may be because I feel so out of control myself. My stubbornness may come from my pain when everyone else seems to be living my life for me. And even though I love the old musicals of the forties and fifties, I hope someone will understand that I wouldn't mind seeing *Rain Man* again either. And while Hemingway and Faulkner are wonderful, there are some classics from my own day as well. And while I can certainly appreciate the Big Band sounds, every once in a while I hope those who care for me will tolerate my need to bop along to some good old rock 'n' roll.

EXERCISES IN COPING

EXPLORING THE RELATIONSHIP

Getting to know the person you care for can help you cope. Here are some exercises to help you get started.

Questions to ask

- What do you think about . . . (world issues, adding more salt to the recipe, raising the children, finances, community news, neighborhood gossip, "The Golden Girls")?
- What was it like when . . . (you were in the war, you had your stroke, we moved to this town, you got married, I was born)?
- Do you remember . . . (the trip we took, your favorite Christmas or teacher or book or friend, the house you grew up in)?
- What do you think we should do about . . . (repaving the driveway this year, renewing the insurance, changing the living room around)?
- What is your favorite . . . (color, food, season, song, movie star, sport)?

Activities

- Photo albums are an excellent way to spend an hour or so getting to know someone better. If there are boxes of unmounted pictures around the house, start to collect them in albums, working with the older person. Don't try to do too much at one sitting; this pastime is an ongoing project. Choose one topic or theme, such as a vacation your mother once took, or separate the family pictures by decades.

Talk about the pictures as you work with them. Tell the stories you recall about them. LISTEN to the story your mother tells, *even if you've heard it a thousand times.* Try to figure out what it is about this story that makes her want to tell it repeatedly. Ask questions. I came across a picture in my parents' collection of a beautiful woman I didn't recognize. Who was she? What had she to do with my family? At first neither parent recognized her, then gradually it came back. She had been a wartime friend—someone they had known only briefly, but now remembered fondly.

- At family gatherings, don't talk *around* the older person and don't allow others to do it either. If the conversation focuses on some universal topic, make a point of turning to the older person at some point and asking, "What do you think about that?" If a historical event is the topic, ask, "Do you remember that time? What was it like? Where were you?"

- In this age of video cameras, consider making an oral history for the grandchildren and great grandchildren. Make the sessions an occasion. Serve tea in Mother's pretty china cups. Help the star dress up for the camera, with make-up or a fresh shave, and hair shampooed and combed nicely. Again limit the time, and focus on one topic; make the project stretch over time as a pleasure to be anticipated. You are under no deadlines here.

- Involve your father on whatever level possible in plans for a special event like a wedding, a graduation, the birth of a grandchild, a birthday, or special anniversary. Ask his opinion. Help him choose a card or gift. Let him DO something even if you may have to do it over later.

- Put some of those TV hours to use. Choose some programs from public TV that invite conversation, play along with the quiz shows, bet on ballgames or other sporting events. Listen to radio call-in or talk shows.

- Find ways to continue old hobbies if your husband still enjoys them. He could garden on a small scale in a window box. Woodworking might be a matter of simpler projects that can be finished with hand tools. Collections can be a source of memories as well as conversation.

- Give your father responsibility—no matter how minimal. Show that he is important and that what he does is helpful. He is a member of a household and contributes to it in a significant way, even if it's only by folding the laundry, setting the table, or advising his grandson on a butterfly project for school.

- Talk openly and honestly about the situation; do not patronize. "I know it must be hard for you since your stroke," you could say. "Sometimes it must seem to you as if we're just taking over, but we really want to make everything okay for you." People appreciate knowing that others are aware of their predicament.
- Share yourself with your parent in the way you shared before. If you talked freely about your feelings, if you were a family who argued and then laughed and made up, if you were a family who touched and hugged a lot, for heaven's sake, this is no time to change that.

Learning to adapt

Take your relative seriously, regardless of how bizarre the conversation. One night my father awoke around 3 A.M. He sat up on the side of his bed and called for me, "Jo!" I heard the urgency, thought he was sick or falling, and rushed to his side.

"What is it?"

"We have to do something."

"About what?"

"Well, the wrong people are taking over the government—we have to do something before they completely ruin it."

Now this is, you will grant me, a bizarre conversation. And yet, he was completely serious, completely focused on his thoughts, completely rational and coherent *on this topic.*

I suggested perhaps he had had a dream. No, he insisted.

As caregivers often must do, I had to choose: I could insist on reality and order my father back to bed, or I could play along for at least a bit and try to find out where his concern was coming from and where it was headed. No mystery there; by now you know I played along.

"What do you think we should do?" I asked.

"Well, I'm not sure, but something."

I suggested that perhaps the answer was to talk to other people, make certain they knew the problem.

"Yes," he said, nodding.

"But it's three in the morning, and I think even the bad guys are sleeping, so maybe we could start tomorrow."

He laughed a little and then shivered. "I guess so," he said and then added softly, "I'm just so scared."

Was that it? Was Dad's worry less about some evil force taking over the government and more about being frail and old and scared? Too dramatic? Well, what do you want from me? It was three in the morning and my father was telling me I had to stop Darth Vader from taking over the government.

"Yeah," I agreed, "it is pretty scary."

"I don't know how to stop it," he said. There was no panic in his tone, just a sense of being one person in the face of an enormous problem.

He was still talking politics, so I reminded him of all the times the country has been in trouble before and how somehow the people always seem to make the right move, choose the right person to clean up the mess. We talked FDR and Watergate and even the Civil War. "Every time, it was the common people who made the difference," I reminded him.

"Yeah," he said and visibly relaxed.

"So, maybe we could get some sleep?"

"Yeah, we'll start talking to people tomorrow."

The following morning Dad didn't recall our conversation, and I didn't bring it up. Of course, I can only speculate about the real story. Maybe he had been dreaming and was actually talking to me in his sleep. Maybe it wouldn't have mattered whether we talked or I simply told him he was being ridiculous and should get back to sleep. All I know is that nobody got angry, nobody felt rejected, everybody got some sleep, and the next day I felt I understood him a little better.

Chapter 6

Riding the Roller Coaster

The course of caregiving is rarely even. After a period of intense need comes a scramble to organize services and supports, followed by a period of relative calm. Sometimes, the calm goes on for months, or even years. Then something new happens, and the cycle starts all over again. Well, not over exactly, for when the new cycle begins, some assistance is ordinarily in place, and the new crisis possibly adds duties, tasks, and responsibilities.

The caregiver tries to promote well-being for both herself and her relative by preserving continuity of routine and a lifestyle that is as normal and undisrupted as possible. Yet, just when she thinks she has a handle on the situation, something new upsets this carefully crafted and often fragile house of services, arrangements, and techniques for coping.

One caregiver's ride

Here is one caregiver's itinerary on the roller coaster over a two-year period:

March 1987. Mother, seventy-seven years old, is admitted to intensive care with congestive heart failure. Once stabilized, she returns home and resumes normal routine with her husband, two years older than she. Her daughter returns to her own home one thousand miles away.

May 1987. Mother falls at home; massive dosages of "blood thinner," prescribed for her heart condition, contribute to the formation of a football-sized blood clot on her right thigh, requiring hospitalization. Her daughter arrives to assist her father and set up home care for Mother. While hospitalized, Mother again goes into heart failure. After transfer from intensive care, depression overwhelms her. Hospitalization lasts three weeks, and upon her return home, Mother remains semi-incontinent and bedridden.

Her daughter sets up home care with the physician's assistance, hires a homemaker-aide to cook and care for both parents, hires a student to sleep in the house at night in case of emergency, establishes durable power of attorney for both parents. The daughter returns to her own home, exhausted.

June-November 1987. Mother steadily improves physically and mentally and fires the student who has stayed at night. The daytime aide cuts back to limited hours. The physician, carefully monitoring and adjusting medication, notes almost miraculous healing of the blood clot.

December 1987. The daughter receives a call informing her that Father has been hospitalized several miles from home, possibly with Alzheimer's disease. When his daughter arrives, his physician reports evidence of multiple strokes over a period of time, with at least one big stroke which, without causing physical disability, resulted in mental damage. Father returns home with some coordination problems. When the family gathers for Christmas, he still cannot remember much. His daughter increases the hours of day help and hires two aides to alternate staying at night.

January 1988. Father enters the hospital again. This time diabetes is contributing to his confusion, and he exhibits further stroke damage. The family decides to begin process of closing the family business, since Father clearly cannot return to work. Round-the-clock help is already in place. One daughter takes boxes of insurance and business papers home with her and begins to sort through them. Other siblings begin to monitor the help and close the business.

June 1988. Now that the business has been closed, Father seems to recover. Suddenly he is more coherent, remembering almost everything except the past six months and making noises about going back to work. Family members are simultaneously elated and devastated: have they acted too quickly in closing the business? They reduce household help again to part days and nights.

October 1988. The family gather to celebrate Father's eightieth birthday. Clearly he is better, but the decision to close the business was the right one, for just as clearly he has lost all ability to compute and make the logical decisions required of a storeowner.

December 1988. The behavior of both parents is increasingly erratic. Mother is leaving all household roles to the hired help. She refuses suggestions for both herself and Father about the advantages of attending a senior center or a meal program. She insists that the help stay 'round-the-clock, regardless of need. Her fear is that if the help is cut, she will be unable to manage alone. Her family hire relief day help. There are now four people employed in the care of the couple.

January-August 1989. No hospitalizations occur but an increasing number of telephone calls are necessary to troubleshoot problems. The daughter visits three times, partly to give the full-time help vacations. The relief day help quits. One night aide is hospitalized. Additional support and services are either nonexistent or refused by one or both parents. Their children now handle all business affairs, write payroll checks, compute taxes, meet regularly with each other and help to construct a workable situation for maintaining both parents at home. At the same time, they maintain marriages and full-time jobs. Father loses an eye to glaucoma.

September 1989. Mother is again hospitalized, this time with congestive heart failure and depression. Her behavior is erratic to the point that the hospital requires her family to stay with her continuously; the nurses say they must otherwise restrain her. After Mother returns home, her anger and depression continue. Her daughter finally forces Mother to see a psychiatrist, who starts her on a regimen of vitamins and sets up regular sessions. The daughter recognizes her own increasing anger and depression, as well as that of her siblings and the hired help. Everyone is burning out.

December 1989. Father enters hospital again for hip surgery and possibly a pacemaker. Mother is noticeably calmer, and more physically well. Christmas is an unorthodox holiday at the hospital. Everyone adjusts. Despite Father's illness, things seem better . . . until the next time.

This case is individual but certainly not unusual. The frequent hospitalizations and the needs of two people for care add drama, but the atmosphere of recurring crisis is typical. What can caregivers do? What helps are available? How can older persons be persuaded to allow those services to be put to work?

Ideas that smooth the way

More about support groups

One of the most valuable services professionals can offer family caregivers is respite opportunities, allowing caregivers to get on with their own lives without always worrying about their relatives, to breathe and step away and perhaps gain a fresh perspective.

Support groups are a vital form of respite, as well as sources of education and information that can make caregiving more manageable if not easier. It does take time to attend meetings. It does require an effort to make arrangements, to make the time. But spending time with other caregivers is important in the coping process.

The first thing it accomplishes is to let the caregiver know that he is not alone. Sharing experiences with peers can be a consolation. You find yourself not only sharing problems, but even laughing about situations that would be funny only to others who are in the same boat. Support groups are also excellent sources of information about new services and programs. Usually a group has a "facilitator," a group leader trained to guide discussion in such a way that it provides as much support and benefit as possible for all participants in the group.

Support groups are widely available. If you are giving care to someone with dementia, contact the local chapter of the Alzheimer's Disease and Related Disorders Organization. If there is no local chapter, you can call the national headquarters at 1-800-621-0379 and ask for information about support groups in your area.

Other support groups may be available for caregivers. Contact area hospitals as well as the local office on aging for more information.

If you cannot find a support group in your community or if those that exist do not meet at a time convenient for you, consider starting a group at work or through your church or synagogue. Enlist the assistance of clergy or the personnel manager at work to facilitate the group in the beginning. The chances are good that at work or during your normal routine in the community you meet caregivers every day. They tend to struggle along without much fanfare, so identifying them is never easy.

Other community services

Other resources can also ease the caregiver's burden. Community programs such as *home-delivered meals* and *transportation systems* specially designed to accommodate persons with disabilities can save time and make life easier. Services such as *adult daycare centers, volunteer visitor programs, and alternative housing concepts* can assist the caregiver to maintain an older person outside an institution, in the community, if not in her own home.

For an overview of services and programs available in your area, contact the local office on aging (see government listings in the phone book), or look under "Senior Services" listings in the Yellow Pages. Make opportunities to pick a professional's brain about such programs. While your relative is with the doctor, talk to the receptionist or other caregivers who may be waiting with you about programs and services. When you confer with the hospital social worker to plan your relative's discharge following an acute illness, ask lots of questions to gather as much information as you can, even if some of the services seem irrelevant to your relative's current situation.

File everything you find out, even if you don't think it workable in your situation. Somewhere down the road, the service may be just what you need. Be sure to include the name of a contact person and a phone number so you don't have to search for that when you need it.

A variety of programs may be available:

- Meals—food delivered to homes or served at a central site
- Transportation—specially equipped vehicles for transporting disabled persons to and from doctors, errands, and activities
- Adult daycare centers—programs for keeping frail adults active during the day while caregivers work, take care of errands, or simply get some relief
- Volunteer visitors—often available through churches or synagogues, volunteers regularly visit the home for a short period of time to give the caregiver a break

- Home health care agencies—skilled services of a registered nurse or professional therapist, usually for an acute illness; other services such as assistance with homemaking and chores

- Legal aid—counseling and advice to older persons and their caregivers at little or no cost

- Home shopping—grocers, pharmacists, and other businesses in some regions still accept phone orders and deliver merchandise

- Home maintenance—many communities offer senior citizens services such as snow shoveling, maintenance work such as changing storm windows and screens, and other home upkeep for little or no cost

- Alternative housing options—a community may provide a range of options including shared housing match-up programs, group homes, congregate housing, or continuing care ("lifecare") retirement communities

- Respite care—nursing homes and hospitals often accept short-term stays for older persons whose caregivers need time out for a vacation or just a long weekend

Other services may include advocacy services for seniors who need someone to represent their best interests; financial planning; health fairs and free programs on wellness and preventive care; or counseling for both the older person and the caregiver. In some communities, social workers privately assist older persons and their families to develop a "plan of care." These geriatric care managers evaluate options and arrange services which they continue to monitor. Such services may be costly but, especially for the long-distance caregiver, may be well worth the investment. Contact the National Association of Private Geriatric Care Managers, 655 N. Alvernon Way, Suite 108, Tucson, AZ 85711; (602) 881-8008.

Building a care plan

How do you begin? Once you have gathered all the information about services in your relative's community, consider the needs. You are in a way functioning as a care manager for this person, matching needs with services. Over time, those needs change, and sometimes services must change as well. A care plan is written in pencil, never in stone.

Start by considering your particular situation. With the help of the information you have already accumulated in the exercises in this book, talk to the physician or social worker about a care plan for your relative. If you haven't done so already, list her needs and match them with sources of assistance already available through family, friends, or community services. Then focus on needs that are not currently being met by you or others.

As a caregiver, you need to be forewarned that your relative will probably resist outside services and enrollment in a community program such as daycare. The most prevalent reasons older persons reject these ideas are that they don't want "strangers" to care for them, and (more commonly though less often admitted) they are afraid that acceptance of services or help from the community is a first step on the road to a nursing home and other institution. Once again, they need to maintain some independence, some autonomy over how they live their lives.

I urge you to persevere. If your relative seems a likely candidate for a daycare program, for example, participation can mean not only social pleasures, but also perhaps the opportunity to renew some old skills and hobbies. I think of one group of ladies who attend a daycare program. Each one of them resisted the idea of daycare when their families suggested it. The first few times they attended, they all seemed determined to prove that this place was not right for them and they would not like it.

They are a mixed group whose disabilities range from the early stages of Alzheimer's disease to stroke, arthritis, and depression. Their average age is eighty; they are all widowed; and most live with an adult child. These days the group is close-knit, even cliquish, some might say. But they have built friendships that go beyond their time at the daycare center. They have exchanged addresses and phone numbers. They call one another in the evenings and on weekends. They share their ideas and their opinions. They mourn the passing of old members and welcome the arrival of new.

They were all shocked and incredulous when they heard that one of their number would not be returning to the daycare center because she was moving to a nursing home. This event was a realization of their worst fear for themselves. The ladies cried and protested the decision they were certain the woman's ungrateful daughter had made for her.

That night two or three of them telephoned their friend at home to express their distress and sympathy. To their amazement, the woman told them that the decision had been hers: she was finding life increasingly difficult in her daughter's home. She had spent some time at the home she had chosen, knew several people there, knew several members of the staff and had decided that this choice made sense for her.

The ladies could hardly wait to come back the following day and share this information with the rest of the group. Any caregiver who has ever had to face the possibility of a nursing home (or any higher level of care) with an older relative would have been fascinated to hear these ladies discussing the options among themselves. In the past other members of the group had moved to a nursing home, but usually some catastrophic event such as a stroke or fall had made the decision inevitable, and clearly the group had greeted each episode as the beginning of the end. Now their friend, whom they considered basically intact, had *chosen* a home. It gave them fodder for conversation for days.

In some ways, these ladies have created their own support group. Ideas and issues that would not have occurred to them before, they now debate and decide within their group. They share information. They ask the staff at the daycare center for further enlightenment. Where is this particular home? Has any other client gone there? Could their friend continue to come to daycare even though she lives in the home?

And at home, they tell the story to their families. "Guess what happened to my friend today? She decided on her own to go live in a nursing home!" What caregiver wouldn't pray for an opening like that at any stage of the caregiving process to discuss the pros and cons of nursing home or other alternative care?

It is nearly impossible truly to understand what it means to be a full-time caregiver. The mental and emotional and even physical stress of the job is difficult to describe. It's a little like a woman trying to describe labor or a ballplayer who has torn a ligament trying to describe the pain. If the caregiver functions well, it may be hard for other relatives and friends and even some professionals to understand that coping day in and night out is extremely hard work.

Many caregivers today are employed outside their homes. They need to continue working in order to pay the bills and make life comfortable for themselves and the person they are caring for. Although many full-time caregivers do not live with their dependent relatives, their responsibility is nonetheless full time. My sister, who lives closest to my parents, once said to me, "I walk in the door from work, and the phone is ringing. There is a problem with scheduling the help we've hired, or someone has called in sick, or Dad has had a terrible night, or whatever. I may spend an hour or more on the phone just putting out these brush fires before I've even had a chance to take off my coat."

Other caregivers describe coming home from a full day at work to be up all night with their relatives. Many caregiving daughters I know are caring for a parent besides a husband and children of her own. Even caregivers who do not work outside their homes are severely overtaxed, with little time for their own lives. "I haven't had a normal conversation with my husband in months," says one of my friends. "Everything we talk about focuses on caring for his dad. Everything in our life is colored by how it will affect Dad."

Caring for a mentally impaired spouse involves the additional trauma of having lost the closest possible relationship with a person whose body is still there. "He used to be my protector," one wife told me. "I relied on him for everything, and my happiness meant the world to him. Now, sometimes he doesn't even know who I am." Those who have never experienced that kind of loss can hardly fathom the enormity of it.

Whether the caregiver is an adult child or spouse, she is sometimes overwhelmed by the devastating realization that some things will never be the same again. It once seemed that Mom would be sewing those quilts forever, but now she can't remember how to thread a needle. Or after fifty years of Dad's lovingly chosen birthday and anniversary presents, now comes a gift chosen by the children and slipped among the others with his name on the card.

At a recent support group meeting, one woman was pouring out her frustration about the utter drudgery in her life. The night before, she had changed her husband's pajamas twice, changed the bedclothes as well, and shampooed the carpeting where he had urinated on the rug, all the while trying to make him understand that a mere one foot away was the portable toilet.

"I used to really love being at home—not working at a job," she said. "I would sing as I worked around the house. My husband and I would laugh." Then she paused for a long moment and quietly added, "I want to hear myself singing around the house again." Every caregiver in the room nodded in silent sympathy, understanding, and agreement.

Still, she had taken one small step—she had come to the support group. In the months that followed she learned how to manage her time and her husband's care in a way that allowed more time for herself. She received the approval and encouragement of other caregivers to try short-term respite care despite the protests of her husband. A few weeks later, she reported that he had enjoyed the respite program. She felt more able to manage care for a while longer, knowing that she could take a break from time to time.

Summing Up

Everyone copes in different ways at different times. Sometimes the method of coping is NOT to cope, to deny signals that something is amiss until action is taken by someone else. Other times, like Scarlett O'Hara, we deliberately ignore the cause of the stress. Even the most successful managers don't manage equally well all the time. Most people report that stress makes them feel a sense of challenge, loss, or foreboding.

These are natural reactions to the pressures of being perpetually on call, permanently responsible, continuously burdened with duties which may be more than anyone could manage. Nothing makes such pressures easy, but you can forestall their nastier effects by maintaining a network of friends and information, and by directing your own thinking constructively:

1. Seek all available information about the situation; part of information gathering is the process of identifying what is really going on rather than just naming the symptoms.

2. Solicit the advice of trusted friends, relatives, and counselors when you have gathered the information.

3. Solicit the feelings and ideas of others who are involved with your situation.

4. Determine alternatives which may mutually benefit all parties.

5. Reshape your own thinking as you must to adapt to the solution you decide is best.

6. Seek help when necessary to implement the solution.

7. Take personal (and positive, and sometimes painful) action to work through the situation and reduce or eliminate the stress.

TWO

SPECIFICS

Chapter 7

Help! Mom Just Walked Out of the House Naked! Caring for People with Alzheimer's Disease

Alzheimer's disease is without question the most devastating chronic affliction for the family caregiver to deal with. In the beginning are the little things—the inability to recall a familiar name, stumbling over words, misplacing things. Gradually the signals seem undeniable. A person may be unable to perform a task he took for granted a short time ago. He may get lost driving to the neighborhood grocery store. Whatever the signals, they are frightening to the afflicted person and his family.

At this point, everyone needs to step back and take time to determine whether the condition is indeed Alzheimer's disease. It has been called the "rule-out" disease, because so many other illnesses mask themselves in the same symptoms. Someone who is suffering a series of undetected mini-strokes (TIAs, for transient ischemic attacks); a person who is severely depressed; a patient with an adverse reaction to a mix of medications or who takes them improperly: any of these people may appear to have Alzheimer's disease.

Before any physician hands you or your family member that diagnosis, make certain that any other possibility has been ruled out. At this writing, a certain diagnosis of Alzheimer's disease is possible only at autopsy after death. So if a physician does a cursory examination without considering other possible diagnoses and says to you, "It's probably Alzheimer's," by all means get a second opinion.

Also, it bears repeating that NOT all old people become senile. The word senile originally meant "old," but dementia is the modern term for loss of memory and mind, and dementia is *not* a normal part of the aging process.

If you are the caregiver for someone with Alzheimer's disease, you undoubtedly have a very hard road ahead. Coping will require work. Sometimes your lot will seem monstrously unfair because you must do most or all of the adapting. You will find it hard sometimes to remember that your relative is not responsible for her or his maddening behavior. If you understand that a person with Alzheimer's disease still relies on coping mechanisms that worked in the past, you will go a long way toward understanding how to care for her. If your mother used tears to get her way, if your husband was a "take-charge" sort of guy, chances are those character traits persist. So does a good sense of humor. The key to your own survival may be to focus on and encourage your relative's personality traits that always were positive.

Even in caring for someone with Alzheimer's disease there are good moments. Consider Elizabeth. Originally from Chicago, she moved to Milwaukee to live with her daughter. She is clearly well-read and well-educated, with a mind that is inquisitive and inventive. She carries a novel with her everywhere, and reads constantly when she is not engaged in conversation or some other activity. So far, she has retained much of her ability to form sentences and speak.

Her losses thus far are restricted to the voluntary control of her body. She needs assistance to stand up or sit down because she cannot grasp the action of bending and straightening her knees.

Elizabeth also recognizes that her memory frequently fails her. She has adapted by asking people to write notes for her as reminders so she can tell her daughter about her day. She is clearly used to participating actively in discussions, and she frequently challenges the viewpoints of others. While she is inquisitive and sensitive to others and their needs, she can be demanding. She is a woman used to attention and does not hesitate to ask for it.

In these ways Elizabeth has retained much of the personality she always had. Her daughter is familiar with that personality, which makes caring for her mother less frightening than if she had suddenly started behaving in a totally different way. They always enjoyed their discussions; in their relationship, each was always free to challenge the opinion of the other.

Elizabeth's daughter, and Elizabeth herself in this early stage, cope in part by knowing how the illness may progress. Stages of Alzheimer's disease are characterized by the following symptoms (though not every symptom is evident in every patient):

- Stage 1—forgetfulness and memory loss; errors in judgment, inability to perform routine tasks, reluctance to take initiative; disorientation about time and place; depression and anxiety.

- Stage 2—wandering; increasing disorientation and forgetfulness; restlessness especially at night ("sundowning"); inability to process information, especially sensory perceptions (turning on the stove, for example, and not being aware it will get hot); increase in repetitive actions and questions.

- Stage 3—complete disorientation and dependence; inability to recognize self and family members; loss of speech; complete loss of control of bodily functions; death.

Being prepared

One of the ways caregivers for Alzheimer's victims cope is constantly planning for the behaviors manifested by the illness. *The key here is to plan but not to project.* This disease ultimately necessitates the caregiver's taking over almost every phase of the victim's life. The best caregiver, nonetheless, is the one who plans for that day but does not act until some event forces action.

Caregivers should definitely screen options for alternative housing, for example, including nursing homes, planning for the day when care at home is no longer feasible. But establishing the options and taking action are entirely different matters. Similarly, a caregiver needs to become familiar with her relative's financial and legal affairs and to establish a durable power of attorney early in the caregiving process. But for as long as possible, she should encourage her relative to continue writing checks, paying bills, and managing his own affairs to some extent, even if that management is cursory and requires a great deal of help from the caregiver.

Caregivers help themselves by helping the victim to cope:

- Communication. Explain to the Alzheimer's patient what you are doing and why; be aware of the patient's unique communicating tools, especially as speech patterns become affected (read facial expressions and body language); listen.

- Reminders. Especially in the early stages, written notes as well as posted signs and labels may help and reassure the Alzheimer's patient.

- Autonomy. Any move that allows your relative continued personal autonomy and some independence is important. Avoid talking about him as if he weren't there, don't allow others to do it either; don't talk down to him; give him simple choices rather than always choosing for him; include him in planning for family occasions such as a wedding, party, or holiday.

- Orientation. Use family photo albums, mementoes, and other details of his life to help him remember the value of a past that becomes increasingly hazy; use calendars, newspapers, and television to help him keep in touch with the present.

- Diversion. Find simple tasks that give your relative a sense of being useful and a functioning part of the household. Repetitive tasks are best: folding laundry, vacuuming, polishing, some cooking tasks, simple sorting, and other similar chores.

Caregivers for Alzheimer's patients must *schedule* regular short- and long-term respite for themselves. Short-term respite means an hour every day that belongs just to the caregiver—a time for reading a book, or taking a walk around the block, or a hot bath or a nap, or doing any pleasant thing. This hour is an oasis, time out from care, without the risk of being interrupted by a call for attention. Caregivers can also continue involvement in social activities; hold meetings in your home when you cannot get out. Talk to friends on the phone when you cannot get together. Take your relative for a drive or walk especially if she also enjoys those activities.

Anyone who cares for someone with dementia understands the need to be imaginative about respite. Whether that dementia is caused by Alzheimer's disease, follows a stroke, or results from some mental illness such as depression, the responsibility of care can be intense. When I travel to my parents' home to give them care, I often busy myself with some major cleaning chore that will help them and those who regularly care for them. For me, that cleaning is short-term respite: keeping busy helps me to cope with the fresh pain of seeing them living such restricted lives. I cook, storing meals in their freezer for the days after I have gone home. My way of coping, however, does not work for everyone. It is important to find ways that work for you.

Long-term respite means regular getaways for long weekends or vacations. Once a month, if possible, the caregiver needs "time off"—at least two days away from the person who needs care. At least once a year, and more frequently as the disease progresses and the care becomes more intense, the caregiver should have a week.

For such long-term respite, the caregiver may go away somewhere, or he may send his relative to a nursing home for "respite care" while he rests at home without any duties. If no institution in your community offers such a breather, ask someone else to take over for a few days or a long weekend. Others in the family may take over the care for a short period of time. If they are unwilling, perhaps they can contribute to the cost of hiring a substitute for a short time. Paid nurses and others are available through home care agencies and other community organizations.

Some caregivers who know what you're facing

One of the nightmares those who care for Alzheimer's victims face is the sometimes sudden and unexplainable changes in personality and behavior. Helen told me the following story about coping with the erratic behavior of her husband, Bill:

"In the beginning, six years ago, Bill would get money from the bank, large sums, and hide it. He accused me of stealing the money and kept one-hundred-dollar bills frozen in ice cubes. He even hid the Social Security checks; some of them were never found because he eventually forgot where he hid them. When I arranged for the checks to be deposited directly to the bank, he went to the bank and rescinded that arrangement.

"I could not get him to go to a doctor. There was a handgun in the house, and I became afraid. I tried everything—talking to doctors, calling protective services, but the doctors said there was nothing wrong with him, and the police said there was nothing they could do unless he actually hurt me. They suggested a marriage counselor. Finally I got help through the social services department of our church. They saved our lives. They found a place for my husband to stay for several months while I straightened out the mess our lives had become. Then I took him home. Over time, he became more docile and, in that sense, easier to manage. I continued to work because we needed the money, but worried constantly about leaving him home all day."

This is only a piece of Helen's story. Recently Bill left the oven on all day and he has begun wandering away from the house while she is at work. Twice she has asked the police to help find him. Despite the fact that her finances were already stretched, Helen has enrolled Bill in a daycare program.

Laura is the primary caregiver for her mother, Daisy, who is in the advanced stages of Alzheimer's disease. She is frequently agitated, and, because her speech is garbled, she becomes even more agitated when she tries to make her point and no one understands. Daisy has been living with Laura and her family for the past three years.

Ruth also cares for her mother, Emma, in her own home. Like Daisy, Emma is extremely confused. She has recently settled into a pattern of mistrust when others, even Ruth, try to help her move from one place to another. Yet Emma, a large woman, must have the assistance to get in and out of a chair or bed, and on and off the toilet. Yesterday it took Ruth fifteen minutes just to get Emma into the car so they could go to the doctor. No exaggeration: fifteen minutes from the time they reached the car!

It is very hard to describe what giving constant care to such an adult is like. The hours, the days, the weeks and months and years of sheer physical effort cannot be measured. Even if we could measure the physical demands, we could not begin to imagine the emotional stress and conflict caregivers must deal with, unless we, too, are giving care. Helen, Laura, and Ruth are illustrations whose experiences typify the lives of many others.

Laura is a beauty with an athletic figure, sparkling sunny personality, and a lovely smile that she inherited from Daisy. Laura takes care of almost everyone she knows—her mother, her husband, her children, her friends. The other day she stopped for a minute to have a cup of coffee with the staff at the daycare center her mother attends. She wanted to talk about Daisy, not because she wanted to dump her own turmoil and stress on the them, but because she was concerned that caring for her mother was becoming too much for the staff.

Reassured that Daisy was a delightful addition to the program, and that she was no more, and in some cases less, challenge than other clients, Laura seemed to relax. In passing, she noted that Daisy's behavior at home was requiring sacrifice of more and more pieces of Laura's own life, such as attending her children's school and sporting events. "The kids don't even ask whether I'm coming anymore," she noted wistfully. "They are so patient with Grandma, and so good, but I wonder what all this is doing."

I wonder, too. Doesn't Laura deserve the joy of seeing her own children grow up and of sharing in their lives as Daisy did in hers? Clearly Laura has some hard decisions to make. But she has done her homework; she knows her options. She has planned for this day.

And Ruth, like Laura, is a devoted daughter. Her mother, Emma, is in her nineties. Ruth seems unfailingly cheerful and concerned, but like Laura, after years of caregiving, she is beginning to wonder. She isn't a young woman herself anymore. "Should I start to think of a nursing home?" For both of these women that decision would be a last resort. They both get teary-eyed just mentioning the possibility. Their devotion is real, even awesome.

It is hard to know what to say to a friend who is giving care and who clearly is approaching a crossroads. Helen's financial situation and Bill's increased need for constant supervision may dictate change, whether Helen wants that change or not. If Emma lives much longer, Ruth may have to consider moving her to a nursing home. And considering all of the lives affected by her mother's increasing need for care, Laura may someday decide that some other arrangement is the best choice for Daisy. But while friends can listen, reassure, and support, they cannot make the decision for these women.

They all need some help. First, they need to give themselves permission for regularly scheduled times out from caregiving. During these brief rests, they need to concentrate on themselves, not on accomplishing chores so that all the work will be done and they can get back to caregiving. They need planned getaways of a long weekend or a week, even if they spend those getaways in their own home. This necessitates someone else, someplace else to take on the responsibilities of care for a period of time. And finally, any caregiver whose duties go on for several months and years needs to get into the habit of periodically reassessing the caregiving situation.

If Laura thinks her children are paying too high a price because of Daisy's demands on her time, she needs to rethink and restructure her caregiving routine. If Ruth is beginning to endanger her own health, she also must find other ways to care for her mother. And Helen needs to remember that there are two lives in this marriage; hers will continue after Bill's has ended. She must plan for a life beyond his need for care.

What these three women need right now is to schedule respite and join support groups to help them stay afloat. Then they must look ahead and plan solutions: What if one of them got sick? What if Laura's husband got sick and needed constant care, too? What if Bill no longer recognized Helen? What if?

EXERCISES IN COPING

TIPS FROM OTHER CAREGIVERS

1. When you communicate with your relative, look for the feeling instead of trying to attach meaning to the words. Maintain eye contact and be aware of your own facial and body language.

2. Accept that the nature of the illness requires constant reassurance about

time, place, and person. Accept that repetition of questions, comments, stories, even whole conversations is common. Accept that there will be embarrassing moments; this is a characteristic of the illness which is thus out of youı control. Accept that Alzheimer's disease is an illness of constant change.

3. Occasionally the simplest solution may be simply to express belief in what your dependent is saying, even if you know it is not true. Suppose your husband insists he wants to go home. You know he is talking of his childhood home. You explain that he is grown now, married, with children and grandchildren, and this is home now. He continues to insist he wants to go home. Your best bet here may be distraction: "Okay. But let's have some lunch first (or get a good night's sleep or wait for our daughter to call), then we can go." Chances are, by the time you have completed the activity, he will have forgotten about "going home."

4. As long as they work, use signs that give information and at the same time reassure. Labels on dresser drawers, for example, may enable your relative to retain some independence in dressing.

5. Don't forget that touching is a vital part of communication sometimes. A well-placed hug or pat on the back can be very therapeutic for someone who is anxious and in distress.

6. In contrast, allow your relative to "take care of you" sometimes by occasionally sharing the information that you aren't in a good mood today, that you could really use a hug yourself, that the person with Alzheimer's disease is important to your well-being.

7. When she is trying to complete a task, take everything one step at a time. To help her dress, for example, lay out her clothes in the order she is to put them on, or lay out one item at a time. If choices are to be made, keep them simple—no more than two: the red blouse or the blue.

8. If he "fights" performing some necessary task such as bathing or going to the bathroom or eating, temporarily give up, allow a few minutes to pass or turn to some other more pleasant activity for a minute, and then return to the task at hand.

9. Always allow plenty of time; a sense of hurrying only adds to the anxiety that is constantly present.

10. In the face of immovable resistance, yield and be honest. You can admit

your feelings to a person with Alzheimer's disease: "I'm really tired and although I'm really trying to understand what you want, I can't. Nothing I do seems to work. I just don't have any more answers."

11. Consider using some background music that your relative enjoys or finds soothing when you're trying to complete a difficult task.

12. Whenever possible, promote his independence and personal control; applaud achievements, regardless of how seemingly insignificant they are, particularly in the middle and later stages of the disease. Even if only momentarily, he can experience pride in something he accomplished. Show gratitude for his help in completing this task.

13. Check the environment—keep it simple, uncluttered, familiar.

14. Understand that many nonedible items can appear to be food to a person with Alzheimer's disease. Soap may look like candy, plants may look edible, small knicknacks may look delicious, even after she has just finished a large meal.

15. What works one moment may be totally wrong the next, and *vice versa.* On some days, the television may be your best friend, entertaining your wife for long periods of time; other times, following the story and dealing with the sound and commercial interruptions may aggravate her.

16. Use calendars and posted schedules to allow your relative to keep track of today's activities, time, and place. Don't work beyond today; she needn't keep up with what's coming tomorrow or with next week's plans.

17. Watch for a build-up of anxiety, and try to relieve it before it gets out of control. Usually there are signals and hints of the cause. If you can't figure it out, forget it. Use distraction or a change of activity to lead the person's thought processes in a different direction.

18. Ask yourself whether the goals you've set for yourself and your relative are realistic. If your standards for "success" are too high, you may harm not only his well-being, but your own mental and physical health.

19. Accept that there will be times when you are at the end of your rope. On those occasions, if possible, call in a surrogate caregiver (even a neighbor or friend) to give you fifteen minutes of time out.

20. Understand that you also have a life; you are a person too. You are doing the best you can in a situation that is fraught with hazards. Give yourself credit for that.

Special situations

SUNDOWNING is the agitation that can be a part of the Alzheimer's pattern as night comes on. Frequently persons with Alzheimer's disease become increasingly agitated in the evening and into the night. Some are wakeful all night, pacing and wandering; some try to leave wherever they are at night.

1. Place safety latches high and/or low on doors that lead outside or to basements or areas where your dependent could be harmed. Safety knobs that slip over the ordinary doorknob and simply spin around when turned may solve the problem of keeping the person confined. (Such safety knobs may be found among the baby goods in department and hardware stores.)

2. In extreme cases, some caregivers have found sensory or alarm devices helpful. These can be especially good when the caregiver needs to be in another part of the house or to get some sleep.

3. Some people have found that it spares everybody grief if the caregiver allows the patient to wander all night if he wishes in a limited safe and secure area.

4. Physicians always advise caregivers to limit daytime sleeping of the person who exhibits "sundowning" behavior. Also, pay attention to the level of activity; "sundowners" may not be active enough during the day.

5. The age-old remedies of warm milk or a cup of herbal tea may be helpful. Certainly "comfort food" is more productive than simply ordering the person back to bed.

6. In extreme cases you may need to hire someone to stay overnight and be up with your relative so that you can get your rest. The good news is that most erratic behavior patterns that accompany Alzheimer's eventually run their course.

AGGRESSIVE BEHAVIOR sometimes occurs in persons with Alzheimer's disease, particularly men. When a person who has led an active, demanding life suddenly finds himself increasingly confined to a routine defined by someone else, he may rebel, especially against the person who seems to be in charge.

1. Keep in mind that the chief emotion at work here is that sense of having lost control.

2. Understand that the anger and abuse are more directed at the situation than at you. That understanding doesn't change the situation but may help you to keep your own temper while you try to deal with it.

3. Acknowledge the feelings at work here: "I understand that you're really feeling upset right now. What can I do to help?" If the answer is "Leave me the hell alone!" then do that, if possible.

4. If there is danger of physical violence, try to isolate either yourself or your relative until you can get some help. If there is any episode of aggressive behavior, remove anything that might be used as a weapon until this phase of the illness passes.

5. Whenever possible, try to avoid a fight. One phase of Alzheimer's disease involves accusations that have no basis in fact: "You're not my wife," or "You're stealing my money." Such accusations can hurt and cause the caregiver to want to strike back: "If I'm not your wife, what am I doing here?" The best you can do is be aware of the potential for such episodes, try to remember that the sick person is not responsible for what he is saying, and try to avoid inflaming the situation further. (See section on elder abuse on pp.153-154)

6. Believe it or not, sometimes good old-fashioned humor can work wonders.

7. If the aggression worsens or continues, get help. In the illustration earlier, Helen found that her husband needed to be physically removed from the home for a period of time. Her pastor helped her locate an appropriate nursing home where her husband lived for several months. When he was able to return home, she took up her role of caregiver again.

INAPPROPRIATE BEHAVIOR can take many forms. Shoplifting may be a problem. Of course, the sick person doesn't realize she is shoplifting, but try to explain that to the store's security force. Another problem may be inappropriate sexual activity, such as masturbating, undressing in public, even attempting sexual contact with others.

1. Keep in mind that your relative is not responsible. Since she is not doing these things deliberately, you cannot instruct or reason with her.

2. If shoplifting occurs, the best thing you can do is get to know personnel. Make shopkeepers aware of the illness and tell them that Dad might pick

something up and put it in his pocket. Try to shop at times when the business is least busy. Give Dad a list to mark for you; the task will help keep him busy and reduce the chance of his taking something. If security people stop you as you leave the store, request a private place and then explain the situation calmly to the management. Offer to pay for or replace the item.

3. In the case of inappropriate sexual behavior, your showing anger or embarrassment may only exacerbate the situation. Remain calm and do not overreact. Look for causes; if she starts to undress, is it because she is too warm or needs to use the bathroom? If the behavior becomes a regular event, seek some help from a physician or counselor.

ANYONE CARING FOR SOMEONE WITH ALZHEIMER'S DISEASE would do well to join the local chapter of the Alzheimer's Disease and Related Disorders Association. This organization provides caregivers with support groups, newsletters, and guidance about the extreme situations inherent in caring for anyone with Alzheimer's disease.

For further information

Coping and Caring: Living with Alzheimer's Disease is a free publication available by writing AARP Fulfillment, 1909 K Street NW, Washington, DC 20049.

The 36 Hour Day by Nancy L. Mace and Peter V. Rabins (Johns Hopkins University Press), has long been considered the "bible" for caregivers of Alzheimer's victims.

The Alzheimer's Disease and Related Disorders Association (ADRDA) offers a wealth of information as well as a national network of support groups for caregivers. Write them at 70 E. Lake Street, Suite 600, Chicago, IL 60601 or call toll free 1-800-621-0379 (in Illinois call 1-800-572-6037).

Chapter 8

Parenting Our Parents

The fashionable expression describing children who care for their aging parents, "the parent's parent," suggests the incredible burdens that sometimes accompany caregiving. Adult children may increasingly be called upon by their aging parents for personal advice, for complicated legal and financial assistance, even for some of the same hands-on physical and protective care their parents gave them as children—feeding, changing, and bathing.

The fact cannot be changed that a relationship between an adult child and parents has a history, which they continue to create until death parts them. For young families, most of the process lies in the future, where changes in direction can occur. But aging parents' relationship with grown children has been established for years, usually for decades. Regardless of the frailty or impairment of the parent, the adult child will always be his child, a fact that colors every aspect of giving care.

I was thinking about this quandary on a recent trip to Virginia, as I sat for long hours filing the numerous Medicare and supplemental insurance forms to claim reimbursement for my parents' medical care. I thought about the problem again when I sat with my siblings, and they told me what they thought we ought to do about our parents and those habits that we all find alarming and frustrating. The dual role struck me once again as I sat on the front porch recalling another time when it was my mother who sat there watching me with my friends. Again I reflected on this classic role reversal when the housekeepers who stay with my parents told me what *they* thought I ought to do about my parents.

And then my mother joined me on the front porch. I had been elected by all the others to "have a talk with Mother" and lay out some new guidelines for her life. The moment had arrived, and I realized that I felt the same way I had twenty years earlier when I was preparing to announce that I wanted to move to Wisconsin to be with a man I might love. In many families I've known, the children can state quite easily what they think their parents ought to do, and the parents are only too glad to consider the advice. But that was never the case in our house. And in that moment, with that thought, I understood that, regardless of the growing list of matters I am called upon to handle for them, they are and always will be my parents. The history of our relationship results in boundaries I cannot comfortably breach to take control for them.

A few days after my return home, I was in the grocery store on discount day for seniors. As usual, the store was busy with lots of older customers. A frail lady and her daughter who was past middle-age were checking out ahead of me. From their comments as they unloaded their cart, I gathered they had come to shop for the mother. When the checkout lady announced the total, the older woman opened a worn wallet and carefully began counting out the bills.

I knew from experience that the clerks in this store have been well-trained, and their patience with older customers is infinite; in fact, they set a good example for everyone who works with older clients. So I focused on the daughter. Remembering my sister, who earlier that week had sighed with exasperation when Mother wanted to buy some trinket at a gift store in Virginia, I waited and watched.

The woman took several seconds to make the correct total, but not once did her daughter move to take over the task from her. Instead, she stood patiently by. She did not coach her mother ("Now you need a quarter"). She did not chide her ("Just give her the twenty and let her make change,

Mother"). She showed no embarrassment ("For God's sakes, Mom, there are people waiting"). And she did not take charge ("Here, let me do it").

She must have felt me watching, for her eyes met mine. At first her glance was defensive as if in preparation for some negative comment I might make about her mother. But then I smiled at her, and she smiled back—two caregiving adult children who understood.

As they turned to leave the store, the mother reprimanded the daughter about carrying the heavy bags. "You should use the cart," she instructed with a parental wag of her finger. The daughter looked back at me, smiled, and rolled her eyes, looking very much like a teen-ager who understands that while parents may be impossible, they are still and always your parents.

Of parents and children

Caring for parents is probably no more or less difficult than caring for a spouse or a sibling. Each relationship carries unique circumstances. Giving care to parents is especially stressful because two people, and perhaps even four, may need care over time. The thought of giving care to one person is difficult to imagine; the prospect of simultaneously giving care to two, three, or even four physically or mentally frail parents is staggering.

Yet, people do it. Women, mostly. Daughters and daughters-in-law, though increasingly men are finding themselves cast in the caregiving role. Some catastrophic event may suddenly draw adult children into the midst of giving care. Or changes in the relationship may progress more subtly, with gradually increasing need for a little help here and a little more there.

However it evolves, the parent-child relationship doesn't end when the child leaves the nest. Their connection may have been forged on conflict and perhaps even unfulfilled expectations from one or both sides. Issues often go unresolved, when the child reaches adulthood and removes herself from them, going into a life of her own. But there are still ties, and emotional baggage, some of it untended when the need for giving care arises.

On the one hand the parent may feel that he sacrificed for the child, and now it's the child's turn. That attitude may never be spoken, but it can be a silent, real part of parental caregiving. At the other end of the spectrum is the parent who works so hard "not to be a bother" that he allows his situation to reach an almost disastrous point before admitting he needs help.

Among the adult children in a family may be several different histories and, therefore, a variety of attitudes toward caring for aging parents. Depending on the sort of adult relationships the children have established with their parents over time, some may still see themselves as children of these parents, while others see themselves as adult equals.

And what happens when there is a history of resentment between a father and daughter, for example, when the daughter has some unresolved conflicts and the father is no longer mentally capable of confronting those issues because of his dementia?

Many parental caregivers have talked to me about their view of a parent when they were growing up. "My father was never there for me," one woman said. "He was always working. I know he did that for all of us, but. . . ." If that father now has Alzheimer's disease or some other dementia, he once again is not "there" for his daughter. How does she cope with that?

Or a son may say, "Dad died when I was in high school. Mom kept telling me that I was the man of the family. I resented that—at a time when I wanted to be having good times with my friends, I had to be responsible. I had to take care of her and my brothers and sisters." Now Mom needs him again. He may feel that this time it's someone else's turn, his siblings. They may not understand how he felt. They may view him as having been an ideal older brother who now seems to be copping out. How do they all cope with that?

More commonly an adult child says, "I live a hundred miles away. I have a demanding job and family of my own. How can I possibly do this?" Not that she doesn't want to do it, but how to manage?

Aside from the history of the relationship, which may not surface as an issue for some time, all caregivers face their ignorance of what to do, whom to call, what's available. And many cannot be physically on site or on call because of geographical distance or commitments to other things such as a job or a family.

When parents are raising children, they are guiding them through territory the parent has already experienced—childhood, adolescence, young adulthood. But when we give care to someone older than we are, we are traveling uncharted waters. We have not been there, so it's hard to know what's normal and what's not. In fact the parent is as inexperienced as the adult child. It can be very frustrating when no one knows what to expect.

And finally, the denial which is common to humankind hinders planning for difficult situations: "It won't happen to me, or them." That attitude may be based on the belief, "My parents have always been active and healthy. They are a very young seventy, a long way from the troubles of old age; we don't have to think about those kinds of things yet, thank God."

Caring for aging parents is an individual thing, or rather a family thing. The histories of no two families run the same. Values differ; expectations of self and each other differ; methods of managing differ. In one family, the simplest episode sets off a chain reaction, with everybody in the family becoming greatly agitated and involved and even a bit hysterical, or so it seems to outsiders. Then that episode ends, and the dust settles until the next perceived crisis. Sometimes onlookers wonder how such a family could ever handle a "real" emergency.

Other families are so laid back that nothing seems to phase them. Dad falls and breaks a hip. Mom is practically bedridden with emphysema. They're living on Social Security. The adult children are all struggling to hold on to jobs and maintain their own families. The oldest son's child is in the hospital; another youngster in the family breaks an arm playing at school, on and on. And this family smiles through it all and makes the necessary calls and tracks to care for each other while continuing to hold jobs, volunteer in the community, and help their neighbors. They never say a word; you'd never even know there was a problem if you didn't hear it through the grapevine.

In between are adult children who worry about their parents, who see the frailties and needs beginning to multiply, who look ahead and wonder what they can do, how they will cope. They hear stories from their friends. Depending on the friends, they may have varied pictures of caregiving: "No big deal. Yeah, we're taking care of Mom; she's great—the kids love having her live with us." Or "They are so stubborn! They won't accept any help from outside, but they expect me to do everything." Or they may have friends who have not yet experienced caregiving and cannot understand the cause for alarm: "Well, sure, he's sick now but he'll get better; things will get back to normal."

In caregiving, things rarely get back to normal. Caregivers generally must create new versions of what is normal if they are to maintain some sense of balance in their lives.

EXERCISES IN COPING

GETTING PAST OLD WOUNDS

So, how does the adult child cope? As usual, coping is more than simply finding emotional support. Some very practical, tangible actions can prepare a caregiver to care for elderly parents and in-laws.

Understand the history of the relationship.
When you were growing up, what kind of relationship did you have with your mother? Your father? What are your memories of their parenting?

How do you feel now when you are with them? Do you visit and call naturally, or is there a tag of "duty" attached?

What parts of the person you are now do you blame on negative parenting you experienced as a child? ("I know I have a quick temper," for example, "I get that from my dad.")

When you were growing up were you able to talk with your parents? To confide in them? To go to them for help?

Do you look at other people's parents and say, "I wish my folks were more like that"?

When you think about the possibility that your parents will need care from you, perhaps hands-on physical care, emotional support, or financial care, what are your feelings? Are you comfortable with that idea? Resigned to the possibility? Resentful? Angry? Unable to imagine yourself in that role?

When you think about a parent dying, what are your feelings?

Today, right now, looking at the person you are, do you feel accepted and loved by your parents? Even if one parent has died, do you think she would have been happy with the person you are today?

Mend fences and resolve old issues.
Impossible? "I can't talk to her about any of this." "It's too late." "It doesn't matter." "They'd never listen." "You don't understand." Maybe not. In some families, it may well be impossible to negotiate a peace treaty; the battle has been too long, the wounds are too deep and bitter. In some families it may be too late; the parent is now old and frail and suffering from dementia. She may have died.

In several recent books, authors, some of whom are celebrities, have tried to work their way through old wounds of childhood. In *Dear Dad: Letters from an Adult Child* (1989), comedian Louie Anderson deals with his anger and mixed emotions about an alcoholic father. Even though his father had already died when he wrote the book, Anderson resolved his own conflicts by expressing his thoughts and feelings on paper.

Using the device of the unsent letter, this adult child was able finally to express all the secret feelings about his father and the way drinking had affected their relationship. A letter, written but never mailed, can be an extremely effective tool for working through old anger and resentment in any relationship. Especially in families, people tend to put things off. "I'll deal with that later," we say. "I don't want to upset Mom and Dad with this. When I'm off and living on my own, then we'll talk." If somehow the talk never happens, the resentment never resolves.

Under the pressure of caregiving, that old festering problem can suddenly emerge again. It may not be a problem between you and a parent at all, but between you and a sibling. And at a time when all the adult children in the family need to pull together, you can relieve some pain by putting old feelings to rest in an unmailed letter.

How does it work? Find some time, some blank paper, and a quiet spot where you are unlikely to be interrupted, and start writing. Try to be very specific in what you say. Focus on one issue, the one that has set in motion these old upsetting feelings.

Write as if the addressee were going to read this, but also as if you had finally put aside all the excuses and decided to be blunt about your feelings. After a time, you will find you have run the course of your comments about this specific issue (which may, by the way, be only one item in a long list of perceived wrongs and problems).

Put the letter aside. Leave it for a day or so. Then read it again. Think about whatever implications you have made that the conflict is all the *other's* fault. Consider whether you have any culpability in this matter, perhaps simply by the degree to which you let it persist in your mind. Consider how you feel now that you have expressed yourself, to yourself.

I have sometimes written such letters and wanted very much to mail them, my anger and hurt and frustration having been that great. But I kept them, reread them, added to them, and over time let it go, whatever "it" was.

If you are not a person who does well expressing yourself on paper, you might try holding a conversation, not with the target of your resentment, but rather with yourself or a trusted friend. If you talk the conflict out alone, you will need to play both parts, which requires you honestly to consider what your antagonist's viewpoint may be. If you talk the issue out with a friend, you might try holding two conversations, first talking out your side, with your friend making only nonjudgmental observations ("I see." "How did you feel about that?" "Why did that affect you so?") Afterwards you can reverse the roles, with your friend playing yours and you playing your family member. Having heard your side of the quarrel, your friend can express your viewpoint, and you can present the case of your parent or sibling.

Admittedly it sounds a little unusual to write letters you never send or to talk to yourself, but this strategy works without doing irreparable harm to an already precarious relationship. Of course, you hope that once you have worked through some of your own feelings, you may more easily express yourself to your relative and understand how her responses trigger old reflexes in you.

Build a health team.

Whether you live in the same community or several miles away, make an appointment with your father's primary physician to discuss his health and prognosis.

Establish a primary health team that includes the primary physician, the family pharmacist, the social worker at the hospital where your mother is most likely to receive care, the social worker at the home care agency (as soon as home care is recommended), and any legal, financial, and insurance advisors.

Give every member of the health team your name and phone number for his records, and ask him to call you if he has a concern about your parent.

Ask every professional you meet what programs and services she knows of for older persons in the community, even those which may not be appropriate for your parents at this time.

Establish a secondary support team for your parents, particularly if you live far away. This team might include neighbors and friends. Do not overburden these individuals or expect too much from any one of them. To a neighbor you might say, "My parents are starting to get up in years and I would really appreciate it if you would keep my name and number and call me if you notice a problem or anything unusual." To a friend of your father's you might say, "Now that Dad has retired, he seems to be withdrawing from everything he once enjoyed. I wonder if you would mind calling him and picking him up for the noon meeting of the Lions Club?"

Get a clear financial picture early in the process.

If both parents are living, do they both receive Social Security payments? How much is that income each month?

Are there any pensions from years worked for either or both parents? If so, will those pension benefits continue for the widowed spouse if the employee dies?

What insurance is in place? Do life insurance policies list the surviving spouse as prime beneficiary? What costs do health policies cover? Do those policies duplicate coverage already provided by Medicare? Do they take care of the 20 percent "gap" between what Medicare covers and actual costs? (See pp. 47-52.) Are home, auto, and personal-injury policies adequate? Do your parents have too much insurance?

Are all savings and checking accounts, certificates of deposit, and other assets set up as Mr. OR Mrs.? (If they are in one person's name or the account reads Mr. AND Mrs., there could be a delay in using those accounts if one parent dies.)

Do both parents have a credit rating and history? Often older women do not; wives have established a history under the names of their husbands but not on their own. If he dies, she may need a credit rating of her own.

Research services and supports.

In short, be prepared. Know what's out there, and what is not. Remember, even when a service or support seems unnecessary now, file the information for future use. There may come a day when you are desperate to find a pharmacy that delivers or is open twenty-four hours; doesn't it make more sense to be able to look in your file than to waste precious time calling a number of stores?

Explore housing options.
There may come a time when your mother or father is no longer able to live comfortably in the present home. The bedrooms and even the bathrooms may all be upstairs, inaccessible to people in ill health. The family home may be located in a neighborhood that is changing, becoming more commercial or more crime-ridden as time passes. The upkeep on a single family home can be a problem for frail older persons. And older people can become isolated from society by clinging to life in the family home, particularly when it is in a suburb where they cannot get out to do errands or attend community events because of poor public transportation and distances from shopping areas and the goods and services necessary to maintain a household.

Happily, the number of options is growing. The trick may be to persuade your parent to explore some of these alternatives. The earlier you begin to investigate options together, the more luck you are likely to have. Attending the open house or other events of a retirement community in the area would enable you to observe the life in such places without feeling pressured.

Visiting friends and neighbors who have chosen an alternative living arrangement also opens up discussion of such options with your parent.

If your parent is adamant about hanging on to the home place, do not despair. There are also options here. In a way, that home may be a real economic asset if part of the house can be rented or shared, and some judicious remodeling and redecorating may actually be all that is needed. In a house where the bedrooms and bath are upstairs, perhaps there is a den and powder room on the first floor. Could a shower be added to the powder room? Could the den be converted to a bedroom? If not, what about the possibility of a "chairlift" on the stairway where your parent could sit down, press a button, and ride up and down the stairs?

Include your parent.
The earlier you start to build your information file, the better prepared you will be. Also the earlier you start to discuss with your parents their feelings about issues of aging such as disability, housing options, insurance, and financial plans, the less threatening those matters are.

Don't try to cover everything at once. You might discuss wills, for example, by saying that you and your spouse are in the process of drawing up wills for yourself. In the course of that conversation you can learn whether your parents have a will.

Pay attention. Sometimes our older relatives tell us very definitely how they feel about aging and its practical problems; we just don't want to listen. If Mom starts to say that she doesn't want any heroic measures taken should she be incapacitated, we may cut her off before she has a chance to express herself. "Oh, Mom, you're going to outlive us all." Trust that these issues are on their minds at least as much as they are on the minds of adult children who are trying to care for them. Listen and learn.

Hold a family meeting.

Invariably one adult child assumes the role of primary caregiver. This person may be the oldest child, the one who lives the closest, the only daughter, or one who plays none of those roles. Even when a spouse serves as the primary caregiver for another, one of the adult children assumes that role if the spouse can no longer manage it alone. Unless that person is an only child, she has the right to expect all siblings to play a part in giving care. If you are the designated primary caregiver, then early in the process, you should establish some ground rules. I have always advised caregiving children to sit down in a meeting without their parents. Prior to that meeting everyone needs to be informed about the types of help that are needed now or may be needed in the foreseeable future: financial aid, physical care, social outlets, help with transportation, shopping, chores, home maintenance, and other necessities.

At this initial meeting of the adult children, I advise everyone to come prepared to discuss what he CAN contribute in support and services. All members of the group should agree in advance not to judge one another at this juncture, but to accept that each member of the group is offering the most and best she can at this time.

Once each person has proposed a list of what is possible, those contributions can be matched against the list of needs. As needs are met by members of the family, they can be "marked off" as problems solved. At the end of the meeting, some items may remain on the list of needs that cannot be met by any family member. Now is the time to discuss services from the community and how those services might be employed to help, how they will be paid for, and most importantly, how the parents might be persuaded to accept help from "outsiders."

It's important to remember, when siblings are making their contributions, either financial or physical services, that the need for each service may exist over a long period of time, perhaps even years. This initial pact might cover perhaps the first year and then be reevaluated at another meeting.

In fact, regular meetings a couple of times a year are important. They enable secondary caregivers to participate in decisions about a care plan for their parents, and they allow the primary caregiver to present everyone with updates on the situation.

As the meetings evolve to a regular agenda, issues such as feelings and unresolved history may come up. If such matters begin to impinge on the ability of the siblings to continue care, the group may want to ask a counselor or advisor, someone from outside the family, to sit in on a meeting and help the group work through some of the stress they feel as caregivers for their parents.

ENCOURAGE PARENTS TO ESTABLISH A DURABLE POWER OF ATTORNEY AND A WILL TODAY

The importance of this action cannot be overemphasized. One of the most frustrating things that can happen to any caregiver is for the care recipient who has managed most of her own affairs to have a stroke or other catastrophic event that causes mental as well as physical incapacity. The process of trying to become the spokesperson for this individual without a durable power of attorney is not only time consuming and expensive, sometimes it is downright impossible.

For further information

Check with your local librarian or bookstore clerk for readings on family communication, living with aging parents, caregiving, aging, etc.

Chapter 9

Grow Old Along with Me: Caring for a Spouse

Shirley's husband has had a number of small strokes. He also is severely diabetic, a combination which occasionally leaves him disoriented. He is increasingly dependent on her for everything. Her health is good, although, at the age of seventy-eight herself, she wonders how long that will be true. She tells me she has not been away on her own in seven years. "I can leave him for short periods during the day, so I just get in the car and go to the mall or have lunch with a friend or go to church. I would never leave him alone at night though.

"There is very little John can still do," she continues. "If I ask him to take out the garbage, he can't figure out the lid on the cans. He cannot do the yard work and other chores he once managed—he's too frail and his mind doesn't work in the way it used to. Anything I ask him to do is twice the work for me, because I know I'll have to do it over. He has good days and bad. . .more bad than good lately. Sometimes he can help with the dishes, but only if I am right there. Everything happens these days only if I am right there, it seems."

John takes a number of medications. A few years ago, when he was still managing his own care, he hated the medications so much that he took the whole day's dosage in the morning so he wouldn't have to worry about it again. At the same time, he treated symptoms with over-the-counter medicines or home remedies whenever they cropped up, behavior that may have contributed to his strokes and certainly influenced his sometimes erratic behavior and confused mental state.

Unaware of the problems he was having, Shirley saw the man she had loved for thirty years become progressively abusive and difficult. He was often paranoid, especially about money, accusing her of spending large sums foolishly. "Sometimes I was sure he was going to strike me," she says, "that's how mad he'd get."

Today John is more docile and calm. In fact, he has gone almost to the opposite extreme, for these days it is his clinging that gets Shirley down. "He calls out to me if I am not in the same room. It's getting harder to leave him alone during the day even for short times." She sighs and adds, "Sometimes it's as if we were both sick."

To love and honor

Many spouses experience a period of mourning associated with giving care, a time for reflecting, consciously or not, on what might have been. As an adult child loses a parent, a spouse may be losing a lover, advisor, provider, and best friend.

When one partner undertakes the unaccustomed role of caregiver for the other, the relationship shifts. It is hard to maintain equality in a marriage or even a comfortable balance if one partner becomes dependent on the other. That shift can cause problems in the marriage even when none existed before. And in marriages that were on shaky ground prior to failing health, caregiving becomes an enormous stress and burden.

A year or so ago, I found a handwritten note in a book I checked out of the library. It was intense in its pain and cry for help. "What do you want me to do?" it began. The writer continued for a few sentences, talking about having abandoned a career to give care. Her emotion was almost visible: "I wanted to do what was best for everyone, especially you—in sickness and in health, you know, but I also wanted something good for me." The note ended abruptly, and I realized it might have been the kind of unsent letter I suggested on page 111.

Still those words haunted me: . . . *but I also wanted something good for me.*

In a marriage, certain transitions are considered normal: transitions in the family as children grow up and go to homes and lives of their own; in lifestyle as a couple move up, settle down, and weather financial crises; in the marriage relationship through hard times, good times, chaotic times, calm times. The marriage vows are perhaps never more poignant than when a husband or wife assumes the role of primary caregiver for a spouse who is incapacitated physically or mentally. *In sickness and in health. . . , 'til death do us part.*

The baggage that goes along with spousal caregiving is heavy. A wife caring for her husband may have thought her caregiving days would end when she finished rearing their children and perhaps caring for their aging parents. In a marriage where the ill partner was the stronger personality the caregiver may fear failure and feel insecure about assuming such huge responsibility; when one partner is still vital and active, the illness of the other may impinge on that wellness.

Increasingly we are seeing second and even third marriages. People who have been widowed or divorced marry again, sometimes late in life. Failing health blights such a marriage if it has not had time to develop the history of mutual help. One widow remarried at the age of sixty-seven. Three years later, she and her new husband were just beginning really to know one another, to put together their life as a couple, and to mesh their two families when a doctor diagnosed his Alzheimer's disease. The woman felt great resentment, especially when his illness manifested itself in angry outbursts and occasional inappropriate sexual behavior.

There may also be an element of codependency in spousal caregiving; both partners become victims of the impairments and demands of care. Too often one spouse's identity is tied up in the other person. In her book, *Codependent No More,* author Melody Beattie enumerates the caretaking characteristics of codependents. Among them, she lists a codependent person's tendency to take on responsibility for the lives of other people, giving up major portions of her own life in favor of answering the perceived needs and wants of the other person. Beattie also notes that codependents often feel resentment when the help offered is ineffective, unacceptable, or fails to make a difference in the situation. She cautions that codependents may operate under a debilitating combination of feelings of low self-esteem, denial, and anger mixed with a need to control the situation, to think of themselves as the only ones who really care, and to abandon their own lives and personal happiness in the cause of solving the problems of others.[1]

Ms. Beattie writes primarily about caretakers of people with obsessive or compulsive behavior, such as alcoholics and drug abusers, but there is also an ingredient of codependency in many caregiving relationships. I believe the potential for such codependency increases when the caregiver is the patient's spouse, because many marriage partners have relied primarily on one another for comfort and other needs.

If your spouse becomes mentally or physically incapacitated, you need to understand the losses that may accompany this situation:

- Loss of independence may be the sudden or gradual result of even a single incident in the life of an older person. A slight stroke may curtail a woman's independence even if she makes a fairly complete recovery. If a man fears going out to shop because of muggings in the neighborhood, his independence is compromised. If income falls to such a level that the smallest purchase requires major consideration, anyone's independence diminishes.

- Loss of control over decision making may accompany the need to turn to others for support and help, particularly in the late years of life. Once decisions in some areas are abdicated to others, a snowball effect may overwhelm the older person. It becomes easier to bow to the perceived greater knowledge of someone younger or more expert. Because a man needs help in one area, everyone concerned may assume that he needs help in all areas.

---

[1]Beattie, Melody. *Codependent No More.* New York: Harper and Row, 1987, pp. 37-41.

- Loss of mobility, a frequent sequel to physical illness, may require the use of appliances such as walkers or wheelchairs. Failing sight or arthritis may hamper one's ability to drive. Fear for personal safety can confine, even when health is good.

- Loss of a home, when moving to a different location becomes necessary, is the most visible in a host of losses. A home is not just four walls and a roof: it is cherished possessions and the familiar placement of them; it is associations with neighbors and neighborhood businesses and services; it is memories created and accumulated within those walls; it is treasures lovingly saved because of huge personal significance to their owner which must be sacrificed in the name of space.

And even when one partner in the marriage is relatively healthy, such losses can affect both. Certainly not all spousal caregivers become codependents, but recognizing such possibilities for loss, and preparing to deal with them may help you understand the potential that codependency might develop. Forewarned is forearmed, as the proverb advises. A caregiver needs to anticipate the pitfalls she may encounter along the way. If Beattie's symptoms of codependency seem to match your situation, I urge you to seek some counseling and help.

Finally, while we're on the subject of pitfalls for spousal caregivers, let's address what I call the "everyone-else-manages-so-beautifully" syndrome. By the time a spouse needs care associated with some disability or frailty of aging, the couple has probably already had some passing acquaintance with giving care in their own or friends' experience.

In every support group I have ever attended at least one wife caring for a husband seems to have it all together. They do it all—work, hold the families together, provide the most personal care for their spouses, cook, clean, manage the finances, deal with the professionals and through it all they seem absolutely calm and serene.

These women always remind me of Jacqueline Kennedy, after the assassination of her husband. Almost unbidden there comes the image of a woman who, in the face of horror, held a nation's hand through the sheer grace of her bravery, her attention to detail, her unflagging devotion to her children. I don't think the power of that image can be underestimated. Before those dark November days, we had seen Mrs. Kennedy as something of a lightweight—beautiful and gracious, to be sure, but beyond that? In a few short hours and in front of the glare of television cameras she suddenly achieved a remarkable presence and maturity.

These spousal caregivers who remind me of Jackie Kennedy intimidate me. And if they intimidate me, inexperienced with the exigencies of giving care to my husband, what must it do to the man or woman who is struggling to stay afloat, who is saying, "I'm not sure I can do this, he managed everything, she always took care of me, how do others do it?"

Don't worry about how anyone else manages. Believe me, in all my years of working with caregivers, I have learned that beneath even the most serene surface, are whirlpools of pain and anger and anxiety. You will do the best you can at this calling, and whatever you do will be based on who you are and the history of this relationship. In short, you and your spouse are unique, unlike any other couple. Just as you have written your own individual story of a marriage, you will now write your distinct tale of caring for the other in your later years.

EXERCISES IN COPING

FACING LIFE CHANGES

Even when mental or physical health declines at a fairly slow pace, the losses associated with aging can stress a marriage. The following list of losses is a depressing inventory. Not everyone must endure the whole agenda, of course; some people are fortunate enough to live their entire lives never forced to tolerate a single item on the list, but the possibility exists. And knowing the possibilities can help one cope, because knowing what might occur can prod a person to plan for prevention or alternatives. The successful coper is one who sees the potential for loss and works to create other options, to exchange a loss for a gain by planning for the gain. Here are some suggestions for action:

Loss of employment

Loss of employment can be devastating. If a person has been identified by his work for several decades, the loss of that role may be extremely traumatic. Even when a person wants to retire, if he has not planned a routine to replace the routine of a job, he may soon mourn the loss; it may even contribute to premature frailty.

Pre-retirement planning is one of the best ways to cope with the aftereffects of ending a career. Even when retirement can't come too soon, it is important to plan activities to replace the hours once spent at work. And, if one person is retiring, but the other is continuing her normal routine, planning is especially important. Whether the retiree is you or your spouse, think now about the following questions:

1. What activities will be the basis of your day when you are no longer going to work? How will your partner's routine change?

2. Are you planning to start a second career or your own business, be active in volunteer work, pursue hobbies you've had no time for?

3. What will your daily routine be? Think through a schedule for daily activity, paying special attention to what you will do during your former work hours.

4. What will NOT change? If only one of you is retiring, the other's routine may remain essentially the same. How will each partner adapt? Does the spouse who is not retiring feel any resentment about the other person's newfound freedom? Does the person who is retiring resent that the partner is still working? If a wife has made a career of maintaining the household, what adjustments will be necessary? Will he help with the cooking, cleaning, and laundry? Will she resent his attempts to change her management? What activities that both partners shared in the past will you continue to share?

5. Does your retirement involve a relocation? To another dwelling? To another community? If you plan to move to a new community, be sure you have spent a lot of time there before you decide. If the new location is in a different part of the country, be sure you have spent time there in the "off" season as well as on vacation.

6. How will your retirement affect the lives and routines of other members of the household?

7. How will your retirement affect the household income, style of living, and economic future?

Loss of position in the community

Loss of status intensifies when retirement or illness accompanies a gradual withdrawal from leadership positions in the community. If your wife served in the community as a representative of her company, another employee will replace her in that position. Organizations' emphasis on a continuous influx of new, younger blood to keep them healthy and working may result in older members' feeling devaluated.

Actually there are two sides to this one. You might become more active in the community as you age because of more time and opportunity for being involved. But if your own health or the health of your spouse curtails your involvement, how can you adjust?

1. Define the sources of your current position—clubs, religious activities, social service organizations.

2. Consider other ways to be involved despite the limitations of caregiving. If you are currently on the board of a local organization, for example, consider inviting the board to meet in your home so that you or your partner can remain active.

3. Look for opportunities for community service and identity closer to home. If your involvement has been at the state or even national level, consider working at the local level.

4. Keep up by staying informed; express your opinions through appropriate letters and calls.

Loss of social position

Loss of social position occurs as a person ages and social roles change. These shifts sometimes result from an individual's poor health or her burning out from the pace of activities. One spouse's caring for another can also cause a shift when the well partner becomes isolated because of the demands of giving care.

No matter how much we may moan and groan about the responsibility of our friends and family to stay in touch and include us, if we aren't getting the social contact and support we need, it's up to us to do something.

1. Even if responsibilities limit a caregiver's activity, she can still remain in friendships through telephone calls, letters, and notes. If there's no time, send out a card from time to time; the stores have all kinds of cards with messages about wanting to stay in touch, or you could write a postcard in a few minutes.

2. In the beginning, alert close friends and relatives to the changes caregiving may make in your life and let them know how important their continued contact will be to you.

3. Invite people in alone or in small groups for coffee or lunch.

4. Cultivate new friendships, especially among people who are caught up in the same caregiving routine you are. A support group is an excellent place to meet and screen such people.

5. When someone asks whether there's anything she can do, be ready with something specific: "It just helps so much when you call me on Sunday night; the weekends get very long, and your call brightens them." Or "Yes, stop by for coffee; are you free Tuesday around ten?"

6. Make yourself and your spouse visible and available to others. Take a walk (if he uses a walker, borrow a wheelchair for the walk); enjoy the yard; wait for the mail carrier with a cold lemonade in summer or a cup of hot chocolate in winter.

7. Reach out to others who are isolated or in need. It can work wonders for someone who is housebound to have some responsibility, some feeling of serving others. In one case, a husband and wife who were homebound because of his illness made it their business to call three other shut-ins once a day, just to be sure they were all right.

Loss of identity

After a man's death, his widow, who always viewed herself and was viewed by others as his wife, must construct an identity as a single woman. If the wife dies first, and she always managed the couple's activities, her widower may become more and more withdrawn. Something similar may occur when illness incapacitates one partner. Other people may assume, moreover, that the healthy partner is no longer capable of activity, when only her husband is not.

If Joe has always been known as the owner of the furniture store, and closes the business, or if Sue has always been known as Harold's wife, and Harold dies, Joe and Sue may feel they have lost their identity.

1. Start now to create your own identity and make it multifaceted. Yes, you are Harold's wife, but who else are you? Are you known for your baking, for your artwork, for your garden? What can you do to capitalize on that?

2. Focus on those facets of your life that make you feel confident and in control.

3. Cultivate friendships and relationships with people who seem to appreciate you as an individual, distinguished from the other members of your household.

4. Take positive actions to enhance your identity. Become more active in a favorite organization, in your church or synagogue, in the local community or neighborhood.

5. Do not give the excuse that it is too late. In the movie *Dad*, the character played by Jack Lemmon takes his wife and goes door to door on the block, getting to know all the younger people who have moved in over the years and to whom he never paid much attention during the years when he focused on his own frailties. When the character dies at the end of the movie, those friends form a strong support group for his widow and children.

Loss of friends

It's going to happen. Friends die, become incapacitated by illness, move away. Some friends drift away because they no longer have things in common; this separation happens between workplace friends, for example. But the breakdown of friendship usually happens through simple neglect and absence of contact.

1. Is there someone you've lost contact with whose friendship you still cherish?

2. When was the last time you made the call, wrote the letter, extended the invitation? Sometimes we keep score, believing that return calls are owed, invitations are to be reciprocated.

3. Have you met people through a support group or other aspect of caregiving that you would like to know better?

4. Are you missing opportunities for developing friendships because you are just too overwhelmed with giving care? One woman, for example, missed the opportunity to develop the support and help of her neighbor when she always seemed too busy or preoccupied to exchange pleasantries.

Loss of opportunity

Loss of opportunities may attend a change in outlook, a sense that the later years are a time to conserve resources, not to take risks. Many older people feel that the time for starting a new business or trying some new adventure is past. Opportunities for trips, hobbies, clubs, and other companionship may also be curtailed by the inability to drive, fear for personal safety, unwillingness to take a risk, or isolation in a rural or suburban area.

First, identify which opportunities you feel are lost: opportunities for travel; for making more money; for living in a certain place; for carrying out specific dreams or plans? What?

Then consider whether the opportunity is really lost or simply postponed. Is it the impossible dream, or is it not knowing how to make the adjustments to achieve the dream?

I have friends who were almost killed in a car accident involving a drunk driver. Aside from the physical scars they will always bear, they suffered mental and emotional scarring—fear and anger and a feeling of impotence in the face of something beyond their control.

Out of this suffering, they established the local chapter of a national organization, Mothers Against Drunk Driving. One of those founders became the president of the national organization. My friends turned their loss into an opportunity; they made a difference on an issue vitally important to them.

1. Is there something you could do that might make even a small difference in your life? Join a support group? Start a support group?

2. Have you considered becoming politically involved in the issues of aging and long-term care? (See Chapter 13.)

3. Have you dropped out of all former activities without considering ways you might stay involved on a different level?

4. Do you really need to give up all the plans you made before illness became a factor? Could you, for example, still take a short vacation, planning

it carefully to take advantage of hotel, restaurant, and other special accommodations for the disabled? If you had planned to retire to another community, is that still possible?

Loss of income

Loss of income is a major problem. People accustomed to a regular paycheck must adjust to a smaller fixed income while the cost of living rises annually. The fear and frustrations about their shrinking margin is compounded by the difficulty of finding a job at an age over seventy even for someone in the best of health. Notwithstanding the ads for employment in hamburger places, that difficulty is a fact.

No matter how much some couples warn themselves that financial life after retirement will be different, the adjustments come as a surprise. And if a chronic illness or catastrophic event adds to the drain on a limited income, the stress increases. If possible, make a plan with a professional financial counselor, before you reach retirement. But even if you have already retired, seek the advice of a trusted financial planner. It is never too late to understand the situation.

1. Begin by gathering all the financial facts and figures as outlined in Chapter 4.

2. Go over this information with your banker, attorney, or other financial advisor, seeking their advice on how best to protect and extend your assets.

3. Be prepared to adapt in ways that may have seemed out of the question before. You may have to make some hard choices of practicalities over sentimentalities. The sale of Grandma's antique bedroom set may bolster your resources. If an expensive and traditional vacation makes a real difference in your finances, you could opt for a long weekend at a less expensive destination and pocket the difference.

4. If your adult children have expressed their willingness to assist you in your later years, it would be very helpful to know in what form, and in what amount that help might come.

5. It may become necessary at some point to consider moving to another home for economic reasons. This decision can be extremely painful, especially for women who see their houses as the place where they raised

their children, and, perhaps made their primary contribution. Such a drastic move may never be necessary, but it is easier to accept the reality if you plan ahead and make your own choices rather than having someone mandate a change.

Consider what could happen in the worst-case scenario, and make some choices about how you might handle that. One hopes that these plans might never be needed, but how much better to have thought them through calmly than to act under duress.

Chapter 10

The Loneliness of the Long-Distance Caregiver

Caring from far away involves some interesting challenges. When you cannot be on the scene, you rely on others for many day-to-day tasks. Monitoring services by long-distance telephone calls and occasional visits is difficult, at best. And each visit can be filled with its own particular triumphs and tragedies.

The Visit

Father:
My youngest daughter is coming today. She lives far away, in a city, I think. I was there. We visited her. Chicago. No, that was before. There's a car. Could it be her? No, her mother tells me it is too soon. I am anxious to see her—something is wrong and she has a way of making things all right again.

Daughter:
The trip is interminable. A bus to O'Hare; wait; plane; wait; change planes; wait; rental car; drive. There is too much time to think, and I never know what I will find. What I hear by phone makes me apprehensive. I dread the trip, not because I love them too little, but because I love them too much and am terrified of failing them.

Mother:
My daughter is coming today, thank God. But it makes me nervous, too. Will she notice that I'm slipping as he is? I don't remember everything the way I used to. I feel such pressure. She has to see that we're all right. The last time she was here she went to look at a nursing home. That scared me. She told me it was for a report she was writing, but that doesn't fool me. I have to show her we don't need a nursing home. No, we're fine here. If I just don't let on that there's anything wrong with me.

Daughter:
I've been here barely an hour, and already I see a difference. It was only three months ago that I visited, and yet he is so different, weaker in both mind and body. Thank God, he recognizes me. I'm not sure I can handle that one yet. But he doesn't know where I live. He covers well, but he doesn't know. And Mom, trying to reassure me that everything is fine. I plan each comment with care, afraid of rocking this already tipsy boat. Mom needs to feel she is in charge, and yet it's clear she needs help.

Father:
She cannot make it all right this time. We are in the eye doctor's office and he is talking to my daughter and me. I understand what he is saying. The right eye is gone—glaucoma. We knew that a long time ago. But the left eye was fine until just a few weeks ago. "Possible CVA," the doctor says. My daughter understands, and looking at her, so do I. I see it in her face just before she brightens and tells me on the way out that the good news is that the sight I do have is 20/20. She chatters away, seriously answering my questions, joking, offering me hope and encouragement. I hear in her voice

that she believes in me, believes that I can cope with this. I don't want to let her down, but . . .

Daughter:
I am becoming the person I warn other caregivers not to become—the rescuer. I work endlessly to find a way for my father to fight this spreading blight that is so ugly in name and fact—multi-infarct dementia. I see that he is vegetating, sleeping many hours and then sitting hour after hour in his chair, watching television. "No," I scream silently within myself. "Not him. Somebody else. Not him." I see that he makes an effort for me, and I feel such sadness and guilt that I am not here more.

Mother:
She wears herself out whenever she comes. She insists on doing it all, giving her brother and sisters a break, she says. She is the only one who lives so far away. The others are closer, and here more often. She loves him so much—has always been his little girl. We love all our children . . . each is special. This one has become our friend and as such, mourns each loss with us. I talk about our coming to visit her and see in her face that this is not going to be possible for him. Then I worry that she thinks I am out of touch with reality. It's so hard to keep up appearances, so she can concentrate on him.

Daughter:
I need to concentrate more on Mom. She always seems so strong that it is hard to realize her need. But I see how she escapes when she thinks I'm not looking—how she shuts away inside herself, silent and depressed, and so withdrawn it scares me. I see her jealousy and anger at the amount of attention given to his frailties, and her sadness at the loss of attention he once paid her. She draws herself together to say, "Well, you have no one but yourself, so handle it. Your husband is leaving you, and your daughter is busy with him; you have no one but yourself." I see myself in her again and again, and that scares me more.

Father:
She is leaving in the morning. Does she have money for gas? Will she have to battle the mountain fog because she is leaving so early? She looks tired, and still she makes me smile and laugh. She helps me to the bathroom and makes it seem like an ordinary thing. This was the one I worried about; she was such a rebel. I thought she would run as far as possible from this one-horse town. In a way she did, but she keeps coming back. I'd better give her gas money; she never thinks of those things. Head in the clouds, this one. My dreamer. She tells me not to worry, but it's my place to worry about all my kids—I'm their father.

Mother:
I never used to cry in front of my kids, but lately, I can't seem to keep the tears down. She is wet-eyed and so am I. She hugs me. We never were a touchy-feely family, but her hug feels good. "Take care of you," she whispers. It is her standard good-bye. I nod. "Be happy," I say, my own standard farewell. We both smile in recognition. I stand at the door and watch her drive away. I wanted to tell her to call when she got home, but the kids all hate that. "Oh, Mom," they say.

Daughter:
Home. Pulled in two directions. That is home and this is home. I walk around touching tokens of the life I have made here. The life they helped make possible through their teaching and believing. I start to unpack, and tucked into a corner of my duffle is an envelope . . . with money for gas.

In an increasingly mobile society, the primary caregiver commonly lives at some distance from the person needing care. Such circumstances generate stresses that include guilt about not being more readily available, anxiety over not knowing what's going on from day to day, frustration from trying to manage services over the telephone and during occasional visits, and the added expense of long-distance calls and travel. That expense is more than financial; it involves taking time from work, from spouse and children, perhaps giving up a much needed vacation to give care.

All caregivers feel guilt at one time or another, and they all feel the stress of constant apprehension and worry. But for many caregivers, direct and constant contact with their relatives affirms that they are doing their best. The long-distance caregiver has few opportunities for such assurances. Visits are often rushed and packed with the activity of handling crises, setting up services, meeting with surrogate caregivers.

A long-distance caregiver must be well informed and organized. More than any other caregiver, she will have to create a network of support to assist her in managing care from miles away. Secondary and occasional caregivers become especially important as the long-distance caregiver depends on them to alert her to potential problems.

The job of the long-distance caregiver is no more or less traumatic than that of the one living near the dependent person. In some ways it is easier in that the caregiver is removed from the daily and constant stress of the role. Nevertheless, there are stringent demands and particular skills associated with managing care successfully from a distance.

And that brings up a key issue: at some point, you will wrestle with the question of moving back to your relative's community or bringing her to yours. If you move back, chances are you are going to be making sacrifices that are too great—your life is important too, and you hope it will go on long after caregiving ends. It's important that you protect your life and keep it vibrant.

Moving your relative to your community is also a dangerous solution. Regardless of mental or physical disability, he stands a better chance of functioning over a longer period of time if he can stay in a familiar environment. No, as a long-distance caregiver, you cannot be there to make everything go right. More than most, you will have to rely on the "kindness of strangers." But, there is ample evidence that care received in the home and home community is more successful than care received in unfamiliar surroundings.

The chances are that, as a long-distance caregiver, you also fall into one or more of the other caregiving categories: an adult child, for example, and employed in a job. Remember that each of these roles shapes and affects you, and every caregiving situation is shaped by the people involved. Your ability to be prepared, communicate with your relative and secondary caregivers, and take care of yourself will determine your success.

EXERCISES IN COPING

MANAGING CARE FROM FAR AWAY

The long-distance caregiver can take several measures to prepare:

1. Know what is available in the community where your relative lives *before* you need to use a service or option. Start a file and keep it current.

2. Start as early as possible to identify potential secondary caregivers, should your relative need help.

3. Contact your relative's primary physician and any continuing specialists, and make them aware of your availability and concern.

4. Finally, your distance from the site of needed care does not necessarily reduce your vulnerability to the emotional, mental, and even physical stresses on-site caregivers experience. Find a support group in your community and join it.

This is the big picture. More specifically, you will need to familiarize yourself with other details.

Locate community services and options

Call or write the local (or county) office on aging (or area agency on aging) in the community where your relative lives. Ask for information, including costs and eligibility requirements, about the following kinds of help:

- Housing alternatives in the area, including group homes (sometimes called "community-based residential facilities" or "board and care homes"), continuing care retirement communities (sometimes called "lifecare" communities), and nursing homes (sometimes called "convalescent centers").

- Transportation programs (be sure to get information about costs and eligibility if the program is funded).

- Meal programs (ask about delivered meals, sometimes called "Meals-on-Wheels," as well as meal sites, and again get clear information about eligibility and costs).

- Home maintenance or chore service (programs are often community-sponsored and offer services such as snow shoveling and heavy home maintenance work).
- Homemaker services (programs where a worker comes into the home for a few hours to help with chores like cleaning and cooking).
- Volunteer visitor programs (often available through religious centers; also contact your relative's church or synagogue about this service).
- Home health care (services that are supportive or medical in nature such as visiting nurse, physical therapy, aides who come into the home to assist with bathing, and similar tasks).
- Senior center programs.
- Adult daycare programs (for the person who is alone or unable to participate actively in a senior center's program).

As you collect this information, be sure you get phone numbers PLUS the name of a contact person. In all cases you will need clear information about any restrictions a service carries (sometimes a person is only eligible for a service for a limited time period, for example).

Identify secondary and professional caregivers

Note who in the community you can rely on to feed you information and assist you in large or small ways if care becomes necessary. You can identify these people early in the process and contact them as it becomes appropriate to do so:

- Neighbors and friends can help in any number of nonintrusive ways. Ask one to call your mother every day just to see that things are okay. Give another your name and number and ask her to call you if there seems to be cause for concern. A neighbor's teen-aged child could be hired to handle the yardwork or other heavy maintenance work your relative can no longer manage. If your relative no longer drives, perhaps a friend who does would arrange transportation to church or other social activities.

- People who see your relative regularly to conduct business can keep their eyes open for you: the mail carrier, shopkeepers (especially in small towns and rural communities where shopkeepers and their customers know one another), clergy, members of your relative's social clubs or organizations, adjunct medical personnel who see your relative, such as the receptionist in the physician's office.
- Other family members may contribute something to the process of giving care when it becomes necessary.

Locate professionals who may help

- Primary physician: contact fairly early, even before a real need for care has arisen; record your address and phone number in the medical chart so you can be notified.
- Any specialist your relative currently consults, who will probably continue to treat him in the future: you may need to reach him in an emergency.
- Pharmacist: try to find a neighborhood pharmacist who reliably maintains records of medications and watches for potential problems and side effects, particularly if your relative takes several different prescriptions.
- Hospital social worker: know in which hospital your relative is most likely to be treated, if there is a choice; if hospitalization occurs, immediately call the social services department. These people coordinate details of care such as discharge and arranging home care that may be ordered; they are also troubleshooters and advocates for you and your relative during the hospital stay.
- Home care agency director or social worker: if your mother's physician orders home care, this is the agency that will deliver that service; workers who come into her home to provide a service can inform you about her condition and needs.

* Private case manager: usually a social worker in the business of managing care, this person assesses the need for services and assistance, finds and

implements those resources, monitors them, and generally keeps an eye on the situation. Insurance rarely pays for a case manager. A long-distance caregiver may nevertheless feel that the peace of mind and other benefits of one person's overseeing the process is well worth the cost.

All of these professional caregivers can help you to establish a plan of care for your relative and to follow it through, even from a distance.

Establish a plan of care for yourself

In every caregiving situation, the primary rule for coping is to take care of yourself, not only for your own sake, but also because you cannot care for someone else if you sacrifice your own well-being. As a long-distance caregiver, you can benefit from the following actions:

- Join a support group for caregivers in your community as soon as giving care becomes a regular and ongoing part of your life.

- Collect the information outlined above and make the appropriate contacts with on-site caregivers and professionals, establishing a relationship that promotes sharing of information.

- If you are married with a family or have serious relationships that are likely to be affected by caregiving, talk with those others early in the process, sharing your feelings and ideas about your responsibilities and soliciting their feelings and willingness to help.

- If you work, talk to your human resources (or personnel) counselor or your boss and get concrete information about your company's policy on family leave time and any support the firm offers caregivers (referrals to services, literature, or counseling, for example).

- Once you have collected information about how giving care at a distance may affect ALL facets of your life, plan your involvement:

1. What is a reasonable schedule for regular visits to your relative's community to oversee caregiving?

EXAMPLE: Let's say you are a teacher, and you are the long-distance caregiver for your mother, who lives 1,000 miles away. Driving there takes more a than day. Flying costs an average of $400 round-trip. As a teacher, you have certain built-in holidays that include Christmas and spring break, some three-day weekends, and summers. Part of your contract includes a certain number of "personal days" you can use for emergencies when necessary. Decide how often you will visit and how long visits will last. Plan which of your times off will be for you and your family. Do NOT commit yourself to every holiday unless you can do so in the certainty that you will not eventually resent spending every holiday with your relative, giving care.

2. How will you handle the need for emergency trips that may arise? (The teacher above might reserve personal days for such emergencies.)

3. Can you accomplish more by visiting for shorter periods more often, or is it better in your case to go fewer times and stay for several days? (Finances and the need for attention to details of giving care will affect your answer here.)

4. What facets of giving care can you handle without leaving home? What is the cost in time, money, and energy?

EXAMPLE: If you call once a week, that is an expense— depending on the length of the conversation you could be adding $30-$50 to your monthly phone bill and taking up three or four hours of your time. Other calls to the doctor, for example, are another expense. Perhaps you handle financial and legal matters for your relative. How much time do you spend at this? Are there monetary expenses such as phone calls, postage, counseling?

5. What is the history of your relationship with your relative? Review the exercises suggested in Chapters 1 and 2. The way you and your relative naturally interact may decisively affect your ability to cope with your role.

EXAMPLE: Carol's mother has always been manipulative. Carol's father died when she was a teen-ager and her mother became very dependent on her for social companionship and emotional support. When Carol married Bill and Bill took a job in another state, Carol's mother played the martyr. Now that she is becoming more frail she begins every phone call to Carol by saying: "When are you coming home?" or "I thought you'd be on a plane down here." She says such things in what she considers a teasing tone, but the questions make

Carol feel guilt followed by resentment because her mother does not seem to recognize Carol's right to her own life.

If you and your relative have a history of playing mind games with each other, you may need more help than you think in coping with caring. For heaven's sake, if caregiving is costing you too much emotionally, get some help! Talk to a trusted friend, clergyperson, doctor, or counselor. If the problem seems overpowering, consider professional help.

THREE

POSTSCRIPTS

Chapter 11

Guilt and Those Other Terrible Feelings

It is hard to know how much to do for our older friends and relatives. Those who work with older people are constantly alert to maintain dignity, support independence, and enhance the quality of older people's lives. But how much is too much, and what is not enough or too little? The point comes home to me constantly in my work at the daycare center, and in my own caregiving.

One of our clients, George, reminded me a little of my father, the way he was always looking things over, picking them up. Perhaps he wanted to see how they worked, or whether they worked and might need repairs. Impossible to say. He lived in his own world and could no longer gather the words necessary to explain what he might want or need or think. Dad is like that sometimes these days: thoughts are clearly there, but expressing them is hard. George had trouble uttering even the simplest wish or idea.

He always managed a slight smile at my greeting and then a broader smile for Gramps, the Wheaten Terrier at my side. Reaching to pet the dog, he made noises of comforting and calm. Then he blinked and looked around as if recalling some responsibility unattended. A serious expression came over his face; *back to business,* it seemed to say.

His illness, dementia almost certainly of the Alzheimer's type, had suddenly worsened. Now he spent some of his days sitting in a chair with a soft restraint around his waist. He lost his balance if he tried to stand, and his vision seemed to be poor.

George had spoken very little even before his condition deteriorated. He still occasionally searched through his wallet for the money he no longer carried, especially when lunch was served. He was used to paying his own way. Reluctantly he put the wallet away, but clearly he did not understand who might have paid for his lunch. He suffered our activities with barely disguised impatience: he was used to meaningful work. One day George went in for the musical entertainment arranged for the afternoon. Often we have sing-alongs or accordionists or pianists play, but this afternoon, a three-piece band performed. They started to play the old dance-band songs of the thirties and forties. Many in the audience tapped their feet in time to the music; a few hummed or sang along.

But George cried . . . wept really, tears streaming down the weathered valleys of his face. A staff member helped him from the room, seeing that he was upset, thinking that to sit in a quieter place would help. He sat now away from the music and the others. The doors to the entertainment room were closed, so that the music came from far away. And still he cried, swiping impatiently at the tears as they fell.

Talking did not seem to help. We wondered whether the music made him sad because he had once played in a dance band. Had a particular song triggered something? He could not tell us. He was not agitated and his crying was not a sob, just these noiseless, heart-wrenching tears rolling down his face. We asked if he just wanted to be alone for a bit and got the clearest answer he had given us in weeks; he nodded his head.

Through the afternoon I was aware of him, sitting quietly alone. I could hear bits and pieces of the music and knew that he could too. But he sat there, staring ahead. We'll never know what brought on his tears that afternoon. There had been music before; there has been music since. But on that day, George cried. Why? It reminded me of all the times we have been working with a client with Alzheimer's disease or some related disorder that leaves one unable to communicate. I remembered my first days at the center, when I learned to stop trying to decipher words and simply read faces, when

I stopped assuming that inability to communicate necessarily meant lack of thought processes.

George's tears took me back to the first time I had heard the fear in my father's voice, the fear that he might not be able to manage, when for the first time in my memory, he asked for help, and my role as a caregiver began. George brought back the years since then as I have traveled back and forth to Virginia, and up and down the roller coaster they call "caregiving."

Later that afternoon I brought George a cup of lemonade and he smiled as he accepted it. "Feeling better?" I asked. And he nodded. But his hand shook as he drank the lemonade, and he looked so sad.

The professionals would probably say I was reading a lot into George's grief, and they would possibly be right. But I do wonder what goes on in the mind that can no longer focus except on the moment and the distant past? What happens when such a person clearly wants—needs—to make a point? Does the need to control one's life just stop? And does the natural reticence of this generation, especially the men, and their insistence on strength, play a part in their inability to express pain, anger, fear, even happiness?

A few days after the afternoon with George, I was talking to my father. The housekeeper had already told me how things were going. I had already learned that Mom was very depressed and not eating. I had spoken to other family members. I knew my parents' situation was neither good, nor at a crisis point.

"When are you coming down?" Dad asked.

His question was a normal part of our weekly conversation. "Next month," I answered.

"So long from now," he said.

"Why? Do you need me sooner?"

"Well." He paused for a long moment as if searching for a thought. "Yes."

"Why?" I asked, still thinking that this was part of our normal weekly banter. (Like all children I never come often enough to please him.) "Why do you need me sooner?"

He paused and looked for words as if I should already know why. "Well, so. . .so. . .you can make everything all right again."

And I thought about George. And I wondered whether his tears had had anything to do with the music at all, or had they simply come from some inner knowledge that things were getting worse, and perhaps no one could ever make things all right again.

Making everything all right is impossible, of course. Still, many caregivers try, and the harder they try, the more they deny feelings of guilt, frustration, and defeat. The afternoon with George, the conversation with Dad, triggered feelings I usually hold in check. I felt impotence at not being able to comfort George, and I felt enormous guilt after that conversation with Dad. Did my parents really need me there? Was I missing important signals? Were my siblings and the housekeepers holding back information? After I hung up, I agonized over that simple conversation. I replayed every detail of my conversation with Mom. How depressed was she? What had I missed? What did I need to do? Could I go down there sooner?

Hindsight is 20-20, and now it is clear that this was just a bad day for both of them. But the doubt is always there: How much is too much? How much is too little? How much can I do for them? Am I doing everything I can to "make it all right"?

If Dad balks at the daily walk that will give him at least a measure of strength, should I keep after him or back off? If Mom resists returning to the craftwork and quilting she once enjoyed so much, is it because she knows she can no longer coordinate those actions? Is it cruel to insist that the clients at the center at least try when they beg off that they are in pain or not feeling up to it? If my brother and sisters have ideas that differ from my own about their care, do I wish they would just let me handle things? Do I think of myself as having "special" knowledge of my parents' preferences and needs?

At times like these, I come dangerously close to codependency. I need to rein in my natural instinct to rush in and "fix" everything; for when I see myself as the "fixer," I close out everyone else. And I shut off emotions and feelings of my own that desperately need attention. When we cross that line from "caregiver" to "rescuer," we put ourselves as well as our relatives in jeopardy.

It's important to allow your relative to maintain some control over decisions in her own home. It's important to listen and seriously consider the suggestions and ideas of secondary caregivers. Even when you disagree. Even when you wish your relative would try harder, do more, not give in so easily. Even when the suggestions of those other caregivers differ from your own ideas of what's best. Even when it means stepping back and examining your own motives and emotions. Even when you must admit that you have gone too deep into the forest and lost sight of the trees.

When was the last time you took a moment to examine your feelings about giving care? Do you think all decisions are up to you? Do you feel as if there were no one else willing to help? Are you living life for your dependent? Have you become a "fixer"? Do you resent having to do it all? Have you frozen out everyone else by insisting on doing everything yourself?

Exercises in Coping

FACING, EXPLORING, AND LEARNING FROM FEELINGS

Feelings. We never do anything without them. Unfortunately, too often we rate them as positive or negative, good or bad. This is unfair—to us. It means we blame ourselves for what may be normal emotional reactions, such as anger, guilt, frustration, unhappiness. Not that we shouldn't take responsibility for our feelings, especially when they begin to get in the way of what we want from our life and for the lives of those we love. Denying our feelings or assigning responsibility for them to others gets us nowhere.

"Bad" feelings

In her book, *When Helping You Is Hurting Me,* Renée Berry Carmen talks about the "Messiah trap." If ". . . you are a person who spends most of your time helping others while your own needs get pushed to the side," she writes, "you may . . . be caught in the Messiah trap." According to Carmen, "Messiahs" often believe that paying attention to their own needs is selfish, especially when that attention to self is placed ahead of the needs of someone else.[1]

[1]Carmen, Renee Berry. *When Helping You Is Hurting Me.* San Francisco: Harper and Row, 1988, pp. 2-5.

Feelings that cause us pain or interfere with our performance are feelings we need to deal with. The feeling, pure and simple. No blame. No guilt. Simply, "I am feeling (angry or depressed or unappreciated)." Once we acknowledge the emotion, we can begin to understand why we feel it. Take anger, for example. Caregivers often experience various degrees of this emotion, from mild irritation to absolute rage. Start by stating the following:

"I am angry because . . . (you fill in this part)."

You shouldn't necessarily accept your first answer. You might want to write down or voice to yourself (the bathtub or shower is a great place for this process) several statements that complete that sentence: "I am angry because . . ."

Chances are you will know when you are getting really close to the truth. One caregiver's litany might read like this:

I am angry because I don't have any time.

I am angry because no one listens to me.

I am angry because everything I try to do backfires.

I am angry because the rest of the family seem to be getting on with their lives.

I am angry because no one is there to help me.

I am angry because nobody seems to appreciate what I'm doing here.

Now we're getting somewhere. This caregiver is beginning to identify the particulars of her anger: in addition to her anger she feels frustration, resentment, even jealousy.

And here is where the responsibility comes in. She can choose either to maintain her anger and its attendant feelings, or take action to make a change. One thing you can count on: if you don't take responsibility to do something about feelings that cause you pain, no one else will.

Having identified the feeling and its possible connections to other feelings, you can start to seek some help. If you want to do this alone, you might make a second list answering the following question:

"What would it take to make this feeling go away?"

In this process, focus on YOUR needs and desires. If you are a person who naturally puts others first, you will find that focus difficult. If you have fallen into Carmen's "Messiah trap," it may be impossible without some outside objective help. In our example above, the angry woman might now say:

I would feel better if I could just have an hour to myself every day without having to focus on Mom.

I would feel better if I had someone to talk with who understood how hard it is.

I would feel better if I had one small victory instead of the steady stream of defeats I've faced lately.

I would feel better if I could do some of the things I used to do for me.

I would feel better if I could count on the others to help without my always having to ask them.

I would feel better if someone would tell me I'm doing a good job.

Now take your list of things that would make you feel better and think of ways to make them happen:

- How can the angry caregiver get that hour of private time?

Perhaps she needs to look at her day and identify some time that could be hers, if she postponed some task of giving care or incorporated it into some other time. Suppose she uses the time after her mother goes to bed for housework. She might do the housework at some other time. Or perhaps she could hire someone to sit with her mother for an hour a day or two hours every other day and use the time for herself. There may be other answers. The point is to consider all possibilities.

- How can the caregiver find someone who understands to talk with?

Now you already know the answer to this one . . . all together now: THE SUPPORT GROUP. But there are other possibilities. Caregivers may falsely assume that their peers and friends would not understand when in fact, many of them are going through a similar experience and probably looking for someone to understand them. She could try calling a good friend and admitting that she could use a sympathetic ear. Not that she should constantly burden a friend with daily moaning and groaning about her plight. And if her friend makes suggestions or tries in other ways to be helpful, she should do her best to appreciate and consider such overtures openly, not reject them with a curt: "You obviously don't understand the situation."

- How can she achieve the "one small victory"?

Undoubtedly she has often succeeded. The trouble is that when we feel down, we tend to dwell on gloomy things. Successes don't fit into the pattern of depression or anger. Now she needs to think about what she has done that's been good, even if her achievements have seemingly been unappreciated. And while we're on this subject, she might want to consider why it feels as if everything lately has failed. This could be a sign of caregiver burnout (see the next chapter).

- What is it that the caregiver has sacrificed or postponed in her life in order to give care, and was it all necessary?

For example, if she dropped out of organizations or activities that she enjoyed and that involved her in a social circle, could she resume some of those activities when the crisis has passed? If she can't get away for a meeting, how about getting involved some other way—working on a phone committee, stuffing envelopes? She might be surprised at the positive effect her return to some "normal" activity has on her mother as well as herself. If she has given up singing in the church choir because she needs to keep an eye on Mom in church, could the minister suggest someone else who might sit with Mom? If she used to play cards, can she invite the bridge club to hold a game at her house? If she enjoyed her work, could she enroll Mom in daycare and go back to work part time?

- How can the caregiver persuade others to do their part without always having to ask them for help?

She may be surprised to find that others have gone on with their lives because she seemed to be managing so well without them and even seemed to resent their interference. Sometimes when we assume a major caregiving role, we do tend to push others away. It's frankly easier sometimes than having to deal with the family politics or with siblings' feelings or needs or ideas. It's simpler to just go ahead and do it. The family meeting suggested on page 115 is a good way to allow everyone to make a commitment to caregiving. And there should be periodic follow-up meetings as the situation changes.

- Finally, how can this woman get some appreciation?

Surely others do appreciate and admire her, and recognize the good she has done. Maybe the respect isn't coming from the person or persons she wants most to hear it from. And the hard fact may be that she will never hear it from that direction. She may have to accept this fact and move past it, enjoying the admiration she receives from others and the pride she has a right to feel about her own performance.

A special note about abuse

Unfortunately, a growing problem in the care of older people is elder abuse. And the time that even a very good caregiver is most susceptible to this situation is when he is overtired, stressed, emotionally upset, financially strapped, and burned out.

Abuse of older persons can take many forms. The most obvious, and probably the first to come to mind is physical abuse. "I would never strike my relative," you say, shocked that such an idea should even be mentioned. But what if the person you care for is confused and in that confusion becomes angry . . . even violent? Physical abuse happens from both directions, in the best of families.

Other forms of abuse toward older persons include financial abuse (misuse of the older person's funds or property); psychological abuse (calling the person names, swearing at her, threatening her, and in general creating an atmosphere of fear, isolation, or humiliation); and simple neglect (intentionally or even unintentionally failing to carry out some aspect of the caregiving role on which the older person is dependent, such as preparing meals, paying bills, or administering medications).

Abuse among older persons has reached such a point of crisis that many states and communities have created special task forces to deal with the problem. And you need to understand that abuse, intentional or not, is a crime.

On the positive side, most caregivers never give way to such behavior. But if you have been giving care for a long time, you may wish to consider the following warning signs that may lead a caregiver to an episode of abuse. Abusers of older persons may exhibit several of the following symptoms:

Resentment or anger, especially toward the dependent
Defensive reactions to suggestions or criticism
Blaming others
Reliance on drugs or alcohol
Neglect of one's own physical health
Prolonged lack of adequate rest

Refusal to take time off for respite
Depression
Financial woes, problems in other relationships, problems at work
Marked personality changes or unusual changes in routine (sudden overeating, for example, or a marked change in physical appearance)

Have you had even the most minor episode of abusive behavior?

- One day you got so furious that you simply left, knowing that your relative should not be left alone for even a few minutes.

- Once you "borrowed" several hundred dollars from the person's account because you felt you had earned it.

- Once when you were totally exhausted and depressed, your relative relieved himself on your white living room carpet, and you shouted obscenities at him the whole time you were cleaning up the mess.

Abuse is not necessarily ongoing. One episode may be a signal. The question is how do you see it coming and prevent even the most seemingly insignificant episode of abuse?

1. Once again, the key is being prepared: knowing the prognosis, knowing what help is needed and where that help may come from, knowing financial and legal facts that will help you provide care with a minimum of surprises.

2. And once again, the second key is keeping your own support network intact. For once I'm not going to insist on a support group, but you must maintain REGULAR contact with friends who will listen and offer encouragement, with other family members, with neighbors and others who may provide even occasional support and reassurance.

3. While you are planning for the needs of your relative and for others you may care for (spouse and children, for example), do not overlook the importance of the cost in good old greenbacks. The pressures caused by insufficient money may result in abuse.

4. Finally, don't just find out about services that can help in the community—put them to work for you. Don't just consider opportunities for respite—schedule it, plan for it, DO it.

"Good" feelings: finding them and holding on

We've focused on anger. This is not to say there aren't a number of equally painful feelings a caregiver may have to deal with off and on as the situation goes on. Guilt is another biggie, as are depression and sheer panic. There's jealousy and resentment. There's the frustrating inability to make everything all right. One or more of these feelings, added to the unpredictability of giving care, can cause us to live under an almost constant cloud of stress.

How do we cope with that? How do we achieve the desired "good" feeling—HAPPINESS—in the midst of stress? Helping you find happiness, contentment, and satisfaction in spite of the duress of giving care is what this book is all about. Most of the suggestions are good common sense.

- Take care of your own health: get enough rest, eat properly, avoid dependency on any "comfort" solution (including food, drugs, alcohol), and exercise regularly, no matter how exhausted you are.

- Maintain as normal a lifestyle as possible for as long as possible. If something catastrophic interrupts that activity, don't abandon it. Get back to that active routine once the crisis passes or is under control. If you or your relative can no longer perform or participate in certain activities, make substitutions. Seek activities that are less demanding, less stressful, but don't abandon all activity.

- Give yourself credit for the really fine thing you are doing. You are a good person. You have generosity and love and other virtues we all need to hear about from time to time. It doesn't matter if others don't seem to appreciate you; you know that you are doing the best you can. And because you are, give yourself permission to continue to maintain and protect a life of your own; occasionally to give in to anger and frustration; to take regular time off; to seek solutions that not only ensure a quality of life for your relative, but for you as well.

- Speak out. You are the expert in this field of long-term chronic caregiving. It is you who can identify what is needed, how it should be delivered, what it should cost. You are the advocate for not only your relative, but yourself and the caregivers who come after you. Share the knowledge you have gained. Build a better system (see Chapter 13).

Feelings are neither good nor bad, though they can be damaging. They can also be overpowering, like my guilt when I knew that I could not make my parents' lives all right again. Acknowledging and examining the variety of emotions that accompany the role of giving care is another step toward coping. Suppressing what you feel can lead to burnout.

Chapter 12

And the Caring Goes On . . . and On . . . and . . .

The ongoing process of caring for someone who is coming to the end of his life requires constant adjustment. There are days filled with the tasks of seeking, implementing, and monitoring services, nights of pure exhaustion, hours of boredom and drudgery, interrupted by fleeting moments of joy, pain, laughter, sorrow, and high drama. The seasons of giving care do not flow predictably one after the other.

As I move into the sixth spring of giving intensive care for my parents, I realize how many times, just when I thought I had it all organized, something threw me. Sometimes it was a new crisis: a fractured hip, congestive heart failure, or stroke. And other times it was the reverse: a medication change that seemed to bring almost miraculous results, a remission that made normalcy possible again. In either case, the change was unpredictable and surprising. Caregiving resembles the weather: just when you think you've seen the last of the winter coats, along comes a late ice storm. And just when you think you'll die if you have to face one more gray, monochromatic day, a crocus blooms, brown grass turns green, and overnight the bone-chilling wind turns balmy.

In the seasons of giving care, summer comes early. In the beginning, the caregiver attacks the role with the vigor of the farmer who knows he only has so many days to produce a successful harvest. The family is still flushed with the suddenness of the catastrophic event or diagnosis and determined that *their* relative shall be different, that they will *make* things different. The caregiver hastens to make the calls, set up services, and seek solutions. Now she gives her all, physically and emotionally. And now, as in summer, it seems important to make each day, each action count; winter may come early, and one never knows how many good days there will be.

There is also a season when the caregiver settles in to realities that cannot be denied. Like nature's autumn, this season offers wonderful golden days when the caregiver looks at her husband and recalls the calm, bygone times, but it also brings ponderous solemn days, when the realities of the present come home and denial of the future is not possible.

The caregiver's winters are those times, whenever they may occur in the year, when emotions weigh heaviest on the heart. The depression, the anger, the guilt, the face-to-face encounters with our own heredity and mortality, the sheer sadness of a single moment.

I had a winter moment the last time I was in Virginia. Because of my father's frequent confusion and physical unsteadiness, it is necessary for someone to sleep on a cot by his bed at night, in case he needs to get up. I was lying there on that cot. He was in his bed. Neither of us was sleeping and it was very late or very early, depending on your perspective of the day. And I watched him lying there staring at the ceiling, thinking . . . about what?

I have long ago faced the reality that whole segments of his life are lost from his memory—the wonderful work he used to do as a woodworker, the people he knew, and the places he visited. And in that moment I thought, "What's the point of a life well lived, of being such an incredibly terrific person, if at the end, you have no memory of it?" What does a person think about on those long, sleepless nights when such huge pieces are missing? Where's the equity in that for a man who gave his best? What kind of comfort is there at the end of life when your yesterdays are pretty much wiped out? That was my winter—I wanted so much the release of crying that night. But I just lay there, the tears dammed behind walls of frozen anger, the world cold and unyielding for this good man and all the others I have known who clearly deserved so much better.

As caregiving comes to seem an increasingly natural process in life, the years pass. Almost before you realize it, you've been in this role for a long time. You have a history to look back on and consider. And when doubt or indecision arises, that history helps enormously. "But remember when we thought this was it," you say, "and then the medicine worked, and she was better than before?" Like the rest of life, giving care means building in hope and finding the courage to move on.

Anyone subjected to stress in a situation where the end is known but unpredictable, searches for something to cling to. In the absence of answers, we create structure, even rigid structure. We cling to what little control we can bring to the situation, resisting efforts by others to change the familiar, even when change might help.

Resisting help, we exhaust ourselves. Insisting on doing it all, we hope to prove the worthiness of our efforts. When others suggest changes, we take the suggestion as criticism. That hurts, which in turn makes us angry and more determined than ever to proceed alone.

In *Burn-Out: The High Cost of Achievement,* Dr. Herbert J. Ferdenberger describes a burned-out person as "someone in a state of fatigue or frustration brought about by devotion to a cause, way of life, or relationship that failed to produce the expected reward."[1]

That explanation certainly describes the cases of caregiver burnout I've witnessed over the years. It has at one time or another, in fact, described me. What was the reward I sought? Approval? Love? Recognition? Self-satisfaction? Living up to a reputation? Winning? At different times, there were different rewards, but the symptoms of burnout were the same:

- Always there was my creation of some idealized plan of action in response to whatever crisis I saw at the moment. Sometimes the crises were genuine, but occasionally my own fears and sense of chaos heightened them.

[1]Ferdenberger, Herbert J. *Burn-Out: The High Cost of Achievement.* Garden City, N.J.: Anchor Press, 1980, p. 13.

- Once the plan was in motion, along came some minor episode or glitch to upset the perfection of my system: a service wasn't available, a helper didn't follow the formula, one or both of my parents resisted. Usually I translated these problems into some sort of personal failure on my part: I didn't get enough information, I didn't give enough information, I didn't allow my parents enough time to adjust.

- At this point, no one except me seemed capable of grasping the teetering structure I had built to deal with the crisis. In panic, I searched for something stronger to reinforce my house of cards. When others didn't recognize the urgency, I either withdrew and sulked or lashed out at them. I became irritable, and my physical health suffered. I believed that only I could save the day, but all I really wanted to do was escape. I was so tired of being the rescuer. Couldn't someone rescue me? I looked around and resented others the normalcy of their lives.

Fortunately for me, something always pulled me back from burnout. Someone who loves me has taken me in hand and made me face the realities of the situation. More than once, a support meeting reminded me that others share my devotion and stress and frustration about the lack of real answers. Sometimes I have sought professional counsel to help me through a really rough time.

When we both began to experience some caregiver burnout a few years ago, my brother and I decided to go for counseling. The counselor and I had spoken by phone a couple of times, and she had visited my parents, so she had some notion of the situation. She had warned me in one of our conversations that it was unlikely we would be able to change the behavior of our parents, given their age. That left the alternative of changing our own. When I passed this wisdom along to my brother, I could almost feel his resistance through the long-distance wires. But when the time came for the counseling session, he was there, a significant commitment since it meant leaving work and driving two hours each way.

Since I had already spoken by phone with the counselor and summarized some of my problems, I sat back and let my brother do the talking. I had underestimated the depths of his anger and frustration, and love for our parents. What we shared with the counselor that day brought us closer together.

She pointed out that we continually tried to attack problems in ways that didn't work because Mom and Dad resisted. "You're spinning your wheels," she told us. "It's time to try something else."

"Such as?"

"Such as backing off," she replied. "Not physically; if anything, you need to visit more. Back off emotionally. Calm down, and let things take their course. See what happens."

In one way her advice was music to our ears; someone was actually giving us permission to surrender some of the responsibility we had assumed so reluctantly in the first place. In another way, we were scared; wouldn't it be our fault if disaster struck, because we hadn't done everything we could to prevent it?

"Your zeal to make everything perfect for them is admirable," the counselor told us, "but it's getting you nowhere."

We certainly couldn't argue with that.

Afterward, as my brother and I ate dinner together before he drove home, I asked him what he had thought about the session. He admitted that the counselor's taking his side and defending his right to a life of his own, without guilt about all the things he could not do, had surprised him.

"I thought she was going to tell me I needed to do more," he said, "especially since she told you we were the ones who would have to change."

"So what do you think about her suggestions?"

He shrugged, still a bit skeptical. "It's probably worth a try." What he didn't say was what we both felt; for all her good advice, she did not know our parents as we did. We both doubted that anything would work.

I spent the next week with my parents. I had ample opportunity to test out the counselor's advice: "Stop confronting. Concentrate instead on complimenting the positives—no matter how small."

She was right about one thing; we had tried everything else and had nothing to lose, so I gave it a shot. And there was a difference. Oh, nothing miraculous. The serious problems I found when I arrived were still there for the most part when I left. On the other hand, I discovered ways to compliment my mother on the things she did well, and I did see a small glimmer of difference. She was more relaxed and easier to be with, less tense and resistant. It was an easier visit than others had been. There were more "normal" times, rather than scenes that might have come straight out of a production of *Long Day's Journey into Night.*

When my brother came for the weekend, I noticed his efforts as well.

It wasn't easy. I could see he was working through feelings that he had carried for a very long time.

Some families steadfastly refuse all suggestions of professional counseling. Many family members are frankly alarmed that anyone might share private family business with a stranger. "I can work this out myself," they say, or "I don't need some shrink telling me how to relate to my own family."

In fact, I had a little of that attitude myself. Having written books on aging, given talks and workshops, and counseled others, I was a little embarrassed to find myself needing help. I, of all people, should be able to work this out, I thought. But then I remembered the old saying that the person who tries to heal himself has a fool for a doctor.

Burnout also happens to people on the receiving end of the care. The losses they suffer increase the importance of control, structure, and the comfort of familiar things, as their autonomy and mastery of their own destiny diminish. When I pause to realize that my parents' resistance often comes from fear, I am less rigid and more understanding. I know that feeling. I see them clinging to old ways, old situations that no longer work, and I understand. These are feelings bred in panic.

EXERCISES IN COPING

HANGING IN THERE

How do you know if you are burning out? Because the symptoms include resistance to the mere suggestion that you cannot do it all, burnout may be hard to recognize. Ask yourself the following questions:

1. Is it becoming increasingly more difficult to face each day?
2. Do you constantly feel fatigued?
3. Are you experiencing physical health changes—sleeplessness, under- or overeating, headaches, vague feelings of poor health?
4. Do you feel as if nothing you do is ever enough?
5. Do you often react with cynicism or sarcasm to the comments of others?

6. Are you increasingly irritable? Impatient?
7. Are you experiencing feelings of isolation? Sadness? Loneliness? Jealousy? Resentment? Boredom?
8. Do you seem unable to accomplish everything, even routine tasks?
9. Is your performance at work being adversely affected?
10. Are your relationships with others deteriorating?

Ask yourself two more questions and be brutally honest in your answer: *Do you deny others' suggestions and offers of assistance because you think they do not truly understand the situation with which you are faced? Do you honestly believe that only you can make this work?*

If you have answered yes to more than half of the first ten questions above, you should consider yourself on your way to burnout. If you answered yes to either or both of the last two, you need some help, some respite, counseling, support, and you need it now.

Support

- Identify your personal support system. Start with those people you feel closest to. Whom would you call to share good or bad news? To whom would you turn for help in a crisis? With whom would you want to share something special? List those people—there may only be one or two. Then list the people who might be supportive on a slightly more formal or occasional level—the neighbor or coworker, the shopkeeper or service provider, the counselor, social worker, banker, attorney, doctor, clergyperson, or others.

- Identify a similar support network for your relative.

- Of these people, who has offered help and been turned down? Who has seemed willing to give some help, but you've never followed through? Who might be approachable for some occasional or even one-time help?

- Begin to cultivate the close relationships you identified. Remember, this may take some work. You may have rebuffed these people, and they may be suspicious or even resentful of your calling on them now. Make a phone call. If necessary, apologize for past offenses. Admit that you have been trying to do it all—there is no shame in that.

- If a good friend responds positively to your overtures, be prepared with some specific way that she can help, should she offer. "It would mean so much if you could call me or stop by for lunch this week," or "Could you come and sit with Dad for two hours on Thursday while I go to the store? It's so hard to take him with me." (And be flexible. If she says she is busy Thursday but could help you out Wednesday, accept that.)

Counseling

- Okay. One more time. Find a support group and make its companionship a part of your regular routine. It is free. Usually it is led by a professional who can direct the meeting and offer good information and advice. It is a source of ideas and education that can help you manage care more successfully. Many groups have "sitter" services so that you can bring your relative with you and leave him with the "sitter" while you are in the meeting. It is FREE.

- Seek out the counseling services of local clergy in your community, not exclusively your own clergy; sometimes a pastor, priest, or rabbi has a particular gift for this sort of thing. It may also interest you to know that many funeral businesses offer professional "grief and bereavement" counseling. Sometimes giving care means living with the overtones of grief and bereavement. A session with such a counselor can be helpful.

- In more serious matters seek the counseling advice of a professional. Sometimes a community or local hospital offers clinics, seminars, or even individual sessions, free or at a nominal cost. Sometimes professional counseling is available on an ability-to-pay basis. Call your hospital social services department, the office on aging, or look in the Yellow Pages under "Counseling services."

- In practical matters such as legal and financial issues, seek the advice and counsel of the professionals available to you—bankers, legal aid societies, university law schools, etc. In matters concerning the system that serves the elderly in this country, seek the assistance of the local office on aging, the housing authority, the ombudsperson (an appointed officer who serves as advocate for residents of nursing homes, and can offer invaluable information to those giving care at home as well).

Respite

Information about respite—regular time off from giving care—bears repeating. You can avoid much of the damage caused by burnout if, early on, you build regular respite into your care plan. To review:

- Short-term respite means some short time EVERY DAY when you take a break from giving care or thinking about giving care. You take a walk. You watch a favorite television program. You take a hot bath. We're talking ten minutes or half an hour or an hour, but make it happen. It's planned, scheduled, nonnegotiable. That doesn't mean you can't be flexible about it, but it doesn't get canceled.

- Long-term respite means regular getaways for a weekend or a week. Many hospitals and nursing homes offer respite care services, meaning your relative moves in there temporarily while you take a break.

And don't forget, there are other ways to schedule such long-term respite. Other family members might come and visit (and give care) while you get away. You may be able to afford to hire someone to stay with your relative.

- There is also respite in services such as adult daycare centers. While your relative attends such a program during the day, you can accomplish work that is hard to do with your relative around. Many working caregivers have found adult daycare an answer to their needs. It is a relatively inexpensive way to provide care and activity for the person in a secure environment. In some communities caregivers have banded together to form care co-ops where the members of the group take turns giving care for a morning or afternoon to their own relative plus one or two others, so the other caregivers have time off.

Burnout happens. The key is to recognize the danger signals, and to take action. Burnout happens less frequently to those caregivers who have established regular routines of respite and surrounded themselves with a strong support network from the onset of giving care. In a recent support meeting, we were discussing the importance of respite. One woman who was new to the group said, "I just don't feel I need that yet." Her husband has Alzheimer's disease, and he seems to be moving toward the more advanced stages of the illness. "Yes, you do," the other group members told her before I could open my mouth. "You need to make it part of your routine now, because one day soon, when you really need it, it will be too late." Two weeks later, we received notice that Dan would not be at the center on Friday. He would be staying in a respite care center, while his wife went to visit their daughter for the weekend.

Chapter 13

You Want Me to Do What?!

I want you to get political about caregiving. I want you to know what's available and weigh that against services that are needed. I want you to write letters, make phone calls, even demonstrate on occasion—because you are the expert in the ramifications of your particular situation. You know more about the personal aspect of long-term care than anyone else. Whatever their scientific knowledge and technical expertise, all the doctors in the world, testifying before a thousand subcommittees, cannot match one caregiver's hands-on experience.

It is your understanding of the realities of frailty that qualifies you to act as an advocate for your relative and others. Who can say how a person will age? Sometimes those who seem the most frail have a powerful will to go on living. Others, who to all outward appearances have everything to live for, just wish it would end. But for many who are old and frail, there is no voice except yours. There is no one to speak for the growing numbers of "oldest-old" individuals like those in the following stories.

Marty, a client at the daycare center, lived his life in a wheelchair, unable to speak, unable to feed himself, often choking as he tried to swallow, unable to control many of his bodily functions. But Marty had a curiosity about people and an incredible sense of humor that he refused to surrender even in the face of all that life had dealt him.

He was always beautifully dressed. One morning he was wearing gray slacks, a crisp white shirt, and a royal blue sweater that emphasized his twinkling eyes. When I stopped by, he was watching the news; Marty liked to keep up.

"Marty," I said, "there's a thread on your nice sweater." And in my usual busybody way I started to pick up the piece of white thread. But instead of coming right off, it seemed to be attached and it just kept unraveling until I held several feet of it in my hand. "What in the . . . ?"

I followed the thread to its source and found a whole spool secreted in Marty's shirt pocket. That's when a laughing Marty held up a small sign. "April Fool!"

To Marty, life was a joy—even a life which he spent in a wheelchair, dependent on others for food and dressing and movement and going to the bathroom. Marty was a fighter. He would do whatever it took to keep going. He could not tell that to legislators planning for elder care. He had to depend on his family and those of us who knew him personally.

And Alma at 93 would put some forty- and fifty-year-olds to shame. She spent most days in her wheelchair too, a result of her age and diabetes. But her hearing, eyesight, and intellect were keen and constantly active. She had a tongue that occasionally stung and a glance that could rebuke, and she had a fierce sort of independence in spite of, or maybe because of, her confinement. Still, there was a softness about the way her eyes mellowed when a child entered the room, the pure pleasure she took in working the crossword puzzle in the morning paper; the tenderness with which she created her needlework and crafts.

Kate was Alma's good friend, but they were not joined at the hip. Though Alma appeared to dominate their relationship, Kate had a mind of her own. At the daycare center, Alma preferred her crafts to the discussions and programs the center offered. So Kate went to the programs alone, making new contacts and meeting Alma for lunch.

Sometimes Kate spoke so softly that it was difficult to hear her. She was a slight, dignified, former nurse who at first glance appeared docile and fragile. But when a fall resulting in a broken hip threatened to confine her to a wheelchair, Kate declared, quietly, but firmly, that such a life was not for her. She preferred walking. And after weeks of arduous therapy, walk she did, with the aid of a walker.

People who did not know Kate and Alma might have seen only their years and their infirmities. They might have missed the spirit, the individuality of these two women. Even well-meaning professionals who are strapped for funding, have too many reports to file, and work in understaffed facilities sometimes find it easier and more economical to plan for the whole group rather than the individual. Some might even wonder why Marty, Kate, or Alma would even want to carry on. For some older people and their families anger is a human response to a calamity that hampers the enjoyment of life. "Why me?" they ask, or "Why my relative?" The people in the stories above had their own moments of anger. But they and many like them faced the world with pride and dignity and a heroic determination to see their adversity through.

Still, those who view the traumas of aging as a burden deserve equal representation. I also remember Sol. In his native Greece Sol had been a leather worker and when he was ready to immigrate, he looked for a place in America that could use his skills. He ended up in Milwaukee. Actually, his story was not so different from that of Marty, Kate, or Alma.

In his new life, Sol married and raised three children, who in time presented him with two grandchildren. Although never formally educated, Sol, like Marty and the others, was bright and well-read. He spoke three languages fluently. He and his wife saw their children through college; one daughter finished with a degree in clinical psychiatry.

Sol was a small but muscular man with an athletic frame and eyes that were clear and curious. His mind was quick, and in all outward signs, he was a healthy seventy-year-old. But after a series of strokes that had left him unable to work, Sol was depressed. He looked at my Pollyanna attitudes with skepticism. Where I saw a self-made man, Sol saw a man no longer able to support his family. Where I saw a man who, with none of the advantages, had nevertheless built something wonderful, Sol saw only infirmity and failure. My truths were not Sol's truths. I wanted him to continue the fight. Sol just wanted to give up.

Choices. We make them every day—even though it may seem sometimes that we have none to make. Our older relatives make them, too. Sometimes they choose to adapt; other times they refuse help. That can be frustrating for the caregiver who is fighting so hard to maintain her independence and quality of life.

Marty, Kate, Alma, and Sol are individuals. Throughout their lives they made choices based on who they were and how they wanted to live. In their old age, their power to choose diminished. Still, they were no less distinct personalities than they had been at twenty or forty, and the choices they made at eighty were no less personal than those made by younger people every day. Such preferences deserve a hearing even when they run contrary to what families or governments may decide is best.

We are also facing choices as communities and as a nation. Where will our health care dollars be spent? Must we sacrifice the needs of one generation in order to provide for another? Can our society afford to provide long-term care for chronically ill people of all ages on such a large scale as we do now?

Too much for you to think about with all you have to carry on your shoulders now? Perhaps. But lobbying for the rights of those who need long-term chronic care, *and for their caregivers,* can be energizing, rewarding, and ultimately sustaining. It can also be a shared activity for a giver and receiver of care.

Every morning at the daycare center, we keep abreast of each other's reality by talking about such things as the date and the season, the weather, and perhaps headline news. I like to extend these discussions to events that are affecting the world or nation. We've talked rainforests and ozone layers and elections in Central America and the dismantling of walls. And as I converse with clients and they offer their opinions, however haltingly, their eyes begin to light and their faces come alive. And eventually I get what I'm after, one or two who cannot contain their need to express their ideas.

Now sometimes those are people in advanced stages of Alzheimer's or some related dementia. Sometimes they are stroke victims whose primary mode of conversation may be a firm and vigorous shake of the head. But the expression is there, if not the words. The response. The desire to be heard. It happens at least once a week, and it never fails to move me.

Of course, my own parents' need to assert their autonomy has sometimes been distinctly frustrating and inconvenient. It would be so much easier if they would just put themselves in my hands and let me do the thinking for them. But even then, they remind me that they are human beings who have not, because they are old, disabled, or frail, resigned their citizenship.

Unfortunately, there is a long-standing tendency in America to lump all people over sixty-five into one category: *the elderly.* One summer night when there was nothing much to do and I was in a vegetative mood, I watched a beauty pageant on TV. One young woman introduced as a student of music therapy, said her goal was to work with "young people and the chronologically advanced." *Chronologically advanced??!!* How come "young people" get to be young and old people get to be "chronologically advanced"? And how old is chronologically advanced, anyway?

Such euphemisms depersonalize individuals who are in need. Legislators can more easily delete the "chronologically advanced" from an appropriations bill, than they can ignore the "old and frail." Programs are created to meet, and sometimes dictate, the needs of a homogeneous group—the "elderly"—rather than offer individual choices for people like Marty, Kate, Alma, Sol, or your mother.

If "poor people used to live in a slum," comedian George Carlin asked recently, why do we now say "the economically disadvantaged occupy substandard housing in the inner cities"? Jargon depersonalizes the situation and in the process desensitizes those with the power to change it. You can make a difference. The story of your caregiving experience is different from anyone else's story. Your older family members are pioneers in this adventure of living longer than any generation before. You are also pioneering as you create solutions for your specific situation. In the field of long-term care, Americans are essentially making it up as they go along, and there is an urgent need for your voice and experience to be heard.

Exercises in Coping

GETTING INVOLVED

What can you do? It's easy to get involved and the time will pay off for you and your relative in the long run. Here are some suggestions to help you start:

1. Join an advocacy organization such as the American Association of Retired Persons (AARP, $5 yearly membership), the Older Women's League (OWL, $10 yearly membership), or another group such as the Gray Panthers

or the National Council on Aging. These groups mail newsletters and other materials about legislative changes affecting long-term care, and provide services and programs for members. YOU DO NOT HAVE TO ATTEND MEETINGS, although you can probably find a local chapter if you wish.

2. Read your local newspaper and pay attention to newscasts on the radio and television, particularly when they feature stories that concern you or your relative.

3. At election time, identify the issues that matter to you and KNOW the candidates' position on those issues. You can find out where they stand by calling local campaign headquarters and asking for a clarification on the issues that concern you.

4. In your file of information, were there services that sounded interesting, but which were not available or for which your relative was ineligible? Why? What can you do to change that? Is it a lack of funding? Does a restriction in your community stand in the way, such as zoning laws that make alternative housing solutions impossible?

5. Get to know other caregivers (yes, a support group would be a good place to start) and stay in touch with them. There is power in numbers; being able to present yourselves as a group to local agencies and politicians can give you some power.

6. When an issue you care about comes up for a vote in the city council, state legislature, or the Congress, write or call your elected representatives to tell them how you feel. It does not have to be a long-distance call; most elected officials have local offices.

7. Urge your local library and religious centers to supply information to and education for caregivers, if they are not already active in this area.

8. If you are a working caregiver, identify other caregivers in your workplace. If there are a group of you, start a support group at work or talk with management about cost-free activities in the workplace for caregivers (noon time information fairs, information available through personnel office, in-service programs with speakers from local agencies).

9. If you are caring for your spouse, stay informed on issues that affect your finances and legal rights, should he need care beyond your ability to provide. It is vital that you protect yourself and your future, especially if that future

could go on for years after your spouse has died.

10. If you are a long-distance caregiver, subscribe to your relative's community newspaper, to keep informed on progress and programs in her community.

Finally, never underestimate the power of a simple note or phone call. The hopeless attitude, "I am just one person—what can I do?" ignores the power of a single voice in politics, especially when you present yourself as a representative of a growing group of voters. A note or letter does not take much time and the writing can be therapeutic, a chance to get off your chest some of the frustrations of giving care without the backing of necessary services.

Getting involved and staying informed is a coping mechanism that works because it gives you constructive outlets for your concern, your anger, your fears. Advocacy gives you a sense of doing something positive, of exerting some measure of control, of expressing informed opinions.

At this writing, the United States is the only modern country except South Africa that does NOT have a national health care program for all its citizens. We are not necessarily talking socialized medicine here, but only a plan of care that would cover all citizens regardless of their age or disability. We need to reward preventive health care and wellness programs rather than focus almost entirely on catastrophic or acute care needs.

You may be surprised to learn that of all the professional and powerful voices in the country on this issue, it is yours that is most needed at this time.

Chapter 14

A Chance to Say Good-bye

I've known Jane and her parents for over twenty years. Jane's devotion to her parents has always been one of the things about her that I have admired, but a few years ago, when we both found ourselves cast in the role of caregiver, I sometimes found it a little hard to take. She was so dedicated, and nothing seemed to bother her when it came to taking care of her parents. At times, when I was frankly struggling, Jane never seemed to falter.

Time and again her father was hospitalized in emergencies. Time and again the doctors predicted he would not make it: his heart was worn-out, and they had done all they could. Time and again he came home, always with greater needs that demanded more of Jane, her sister, and her mother. Time and again Jane came to me for advice. "How do we qualify for home care?" she asked. "He still needs so much care but the hospital is discharging him tomorrow. What can we do? My mother's own health is being jeopardized."

And time and again I put on my professional garb and told her whom to contact, what to ask of the doctor and discharge planner, how to find support and help for her mother. Like my own parents, Jane's parents sometimes listened to the advice she brought them, but more often, particularly her father rejected or only grudgingly tolerated the services she tried to put into place for them.

Jane nevertheless went gamely on, a Sandwich Generation lady trying to preserve her own marriage, raise two teen-agers, maintain a needed full-time job, manage her own household, and fill in as primary caregiver more and more often as her mother withdrew, burned out by the minute-to-minute care needed by Jane's father.

Imagine my surprise one evening when Jane suddenly admitted to me, "Sometimes I wish he would just go ahead and die."

This woman had idolized her father, always speaking of him with respect that bordered on reverence. Yet, strained by the repeated episodes of acute illness, which had been followed by long periods of constant care, with no letup until the next crisis occurred, Jane had reached a new stage in her caregiving.

As soon as the words were out of her mouth, she professed her horror at having said them. "I feel so guilty even thinking such a thing. But he's so sick and his life is just on hold and so is my mother's. She deserves to be able to live her own life, not his. She's been living his for years now. And he's so unhappy and depressed."

I understood what she was feeling. Professionally I had seen it many times before—the anger at the situation followed almost immediately by guilt for having blamed a sick man. I had not only seen it, but had also felt it. For I, who always professed that I wanted every possible measure to keep my loved ones alive, unless they wished otherwise, had come to understand the rationale for ordering, "Do not resuscitate." Just like my friend Jane, I too had whispered in the dark, "Sometimes I wish . . ."

Jane is not only mourning the loss of valuable time in her mother's life; she mourns for herself and the pieces of her life that have had to be neglected in order to care for her father. And because she is naturally a giving person, she feels her thoughts are wrong, selfish, and unworthy. She is quite certain that she is "bad" to think such a thought, much less say it out loud.

Her sense of loss is sometimes so strong she has to justify herself by explaining that her anger comes from seeing her mother cheated. She cannot yet express the strains on her own life and her anger at that.

The emotional ravages of caregiving differ according to the

circumstances and the persons involved. Some accept the reality and devote themselves to the challenge. Others feel surprise as the tasks increase and the time frame lengthens. For some that surprise becomes resentment leading to anger leading to remorse and guilt.

Elizabeth Kubler-Ross made famous the stages of dying, from anger to acceptance. Many who work professionally with caregivers notice in them similar emotional stages, particularly when illnesses drag on and worsen over a period of years.

"Sometimes I wish . . ." is not a blasphemy. It is rather a cry for help. It is reaching a new stage and not being sure of the ability to go much further. One hopes that the caregiver can allow himself to set limits without guilt and say, "Other facets of my life need and deserve my attention. I cannot maintain the level of good care I have given without allowing myself to attend to those other parts of my life as well."

At a recent meeting of our support group for family caregivers, we heard a grief counselor for a local funeral home chain. Tom Nietzche is a pleasant, outgoing man who approaches life with a positive attitude and a keen sense of humor. While he usually counsels families who have experienced a death, he had some insights for caregivers as well.

He spoke about various levels of loss. Even if nobody else attaches monetary or other value to one's cherished possession, one feels its loss nonetheless. And all of the people in the group were experiencing losses of a more serious nature: the loss of a companion, of someone to share decisions, of friends who have backed away in the face of an illness. Nodding my head, I looked around the table and noted that everyone was nodding in agreement.

"Recognition of loss leads to grieving," Tom said. The idea that people normally pass through stages of grief no longer persuaded him, though; he had seen too many people remain in one stage, skip stages altogether, or mix them all up, to think the theory a useful tool for coping. But his message was clear: the grieving process is not only okay, it's necessary and unavoidable.

Tom said a lot of things that afternoon that made us all feel better about the job we were doing. Understanding our loss and subsequent grieving can actually give us a sense of control, he said, something caregivers constantly are in short supply of.

As he spoke, I looked around the table. It was a small group; half of us were staff, but all of us caregivers. I thought about the family members who were not there. One man had been attending this group for years. His wife had moved to a nursing home a couple of days before, and I felt the loss of his absence. Tom's insights would have comforted him during a rough time.

And I asked Tom whether, offering families support and counsel, he ever experiences rejection. Real rejection has happened only once, he told me. Many families express their appreciation for the program, but prefer to work things out within their family or religious center; we hear that sometimes, too. But once, he said, he called on a widower who closed the door in Tom's face, announcing that he didn't need any help. Tom knew the man had no close family and was basically alone, needing help more than others, but there was nothing Tom could do, except be there if the man ever decided to call.

"Grief does not get resolved," Tom told us. "It gets reconciled." Then he asked a question: was there any possible way to avoid loss and subsequent grief?

The room was quiet for only a second before one woman said, "Yes. Die early."

We all started to laugh, even the woman who had spoken. Our laughter was a relief; we had all begun to feel the burden of our caring.

"Well, that's one way," Tom agreed with a chuckle. "I was thinking of another way: not to love."

We all know people, maybe even ourselves, who have become so upset that they swore off ever loving or giving of themselves again. They simply announced that they would never again be vulnerable to loss and hurt. After a day or two, most of us think better of such a resolution.

I looked around the room again and saw that we were all thinking about a life without love. Would our lives have been easier, happier, less vulnerable had we never become involved in caregiving? Possibly. But they certainly would not have been as rich, fulfilling, or productive. We have all learned things through giving care, things about who we are, how we function in crisis, how we cope. We have also learned a thing or two about love. There have been surprises. There have been defeats. There have been tears, and there has been laughter.

Exercises in Coping

WHEN IT BECOMES NECESSARY TO LET GO

There will come a time in your giving care when it is necessary to let go. Needing more than you can physically provide, your relative may move into a nursing home or other care facility. He may die. If the person you love and care for is a victim of dementia, either Alzheimer's or a related illness, the process of letting go may be drawn out over a long period of time. He may reach a stage where he no longer recognizes you, can no longer speak with you, or in some other way becomes more of a stranger as time goes by.

Coping with caring also includes coping with saying good-bye. Too often, when a frail older relative dies or moves, the caregiver's life falls apart. Most often this crisis occurs because, in the zeal to do the best possible job, the caregiver has sacrificed many strands of her life, giving up friends and relationships, leaving jobs, changing habits to focus on the person in need.

In any caregiving situation, there are always two people in need of care—the person receiving care and the person giving it. You. The most important message in this book is this one:

If you do not take care of your own needs as well as those of the person you love, when that person no longer needs your intensive caregiving, you will find yourself with the formidable task of having to rebuild (sometimes from scratch) a life of your own.

When the time comes that your role of caregiver diminishes or ends, will you be ready to move on with your own life? Will you have in place the support you need in friends and activities and meaningful ventures? Are you working now to sustain a future for yourself even while you are trying to sustain a present for your relative?

No time, you say? I'll think about that tomorrow, you say? Make time and think about it every day. As in other matters, preparation is a key to coping. Here are some exercises to help you get ready for saying good-bye.

Wellness

During the process of giving care, do not neglect (or put on hold) your own health. You already know the basics: good nutrition, regular exercise, scheduled check-ups, limited intake of drugs, alcohol, and "comfort" foods, opportunities for socializing, and planned respite breaks from giving care.

Planning

During the process of planning for the person who needs care, plan for yourself as well.

- Make financial and legal arrangements to protect your resources in the likely event you outlive your dependent.
- If you must leave your job, consider other alternatives that would help you to maintain a work record if you wish to return to regular employment once you are no longer giving care.
- Explore opportunities for a second career or a career at home that could provide income for you.
- Maintain your membership in groups that you enjoy and that will be a source of activity for you when you are no longer giving care.
- Keep yourself informed and alert for changes in policy and programming that may affect your future when your relative dies or is being cared for in a different setting.
- If her illness is a progressive one, recognize that leave-taking may come in stages; deal with each stage as it occurs.
- If her illness is a progressive one, recognize that the time will come when you may not be able to be all things to her. You do neither her nor yourself any favors by managing care alone beyond your ability to do so.
- If she moves to a nursing home or a different care setting, understand that your role has not ended. It has simply changed. Perhaps now you can focus more on giving the love and support you did not have time for in the past because of the sheer physical demands.

Feelings

Understand that you will experience a range of feelings during the process of saying good-bye to your role as caregiver. If that role ends suddenly, emotions may differ from those experienced during a gradual process of letting go.

- Seek regular counseling with clergy, a professional counselor, trusted friend, or support group.
- Look for workshops or other aids to understand the feelings you may experience.
- Ask your librarian or bookstore clerk to recommend books that may help you through this difficult time.
- Accept support and help from friends and others.
- Understand that grief when caregiving ends or changes is normal. Give yourself time and permission to mourn.

Getting on with it

It being life—yours. Once again you have choices, one of them being not to do anything. A period of rest may enable you to mourn the passing of this important and demanding phase of your life. But grief that goes on and on is unhealthy. You need to reach a point where slowly but surely you move on.

- Think about the different roles you have played in your life. Some of them, such as parenting, followed a natural progression that included an ending, when the need for intense effort had diminished.
- Establish a daily routine for yourself now that fills the time you used to spend in giving care.
- Assess the elements of your life-giving care that were most impaired, and set about repairing or rehabilitating them.
- Take it day by day.
- Above all, give yourself credit for what you have accomplished, what you have meant in the life of your relative, what giving care has given you in strength and growth, and be proud of the courage in your perseverance.

Care can seem so easy to people who aren't giving it. "What do you do?" a friend asks. "I take care of my mother." What does that mean? Does it mean she lives with you? Does it mean you drive her to the doctor? Does it mean you give her some occasional support and help? Or does it mean you do almost everything from shopping to administering medications, from dressing her to helping her to the bathroom? And how has that role changed over time? And how might it yet change in the future?

Caregiving is one of those tough experiences in life that is hard to explain to anyone who has never been there. Through the years I have learned so much that I never knew or understood until I became a caregiver:

I never knew regret until one day I realized I had missed the opportunity to really get to know my stroke-ridden father's thoughts and feelings about aging and his life.

I never knew frustration until I ran into a national health care system that penalized rather than rewarded efforts to give care outside of an institution.

I never knew anger until time and again all my best efforts to make life easier and more rewarding for my parents were rejected . . . mostly by them . . . mostly out of fear of losing independence, which is what they lost anyway.

I never knew desertion until I realized that, one by one, others were distancing themselves from the "situation."

I never knew shame until the day I admitted out loud that, the way things were going, it might be better if my parents died.

I never knew stress until I felt my parents turning to me to make it all better again and again and again.

I never knew sadness until the day I first cleaned up after my father's incontinence, and he was embarrassed and so was I, and all I could think to do was to chatter away so neither of us would cry.

I never knew heartbreak until the first time I realized that my father no longer comprehended that I lived away from "home."

I never knew defeat until the weeks and months and years passed and nothing I did could truly improve conditions for long.

I never knew guilt until I began to be torn between my parents' needs and my own.

But also,
I never knew strength until the day I realized I had been giving care for five years and had not yet broken.

I never knew self-respect until the day someone said, "Whose approval are you seeking by going on with this; what are you getting out of it?" I knew that the answer to that question had nothing to do with doing something for personal gain; it had to do with doing something because it was right.

I never knew faith until I prayed at odd times about insane things and got answers.

I never knew courage until the first day I spoke up for people who could not speak up for themselves.

And I never really had the slightest understanding of what it took to be a survivor in even the most basic sense until I became a caregiver.

About the Author

Jo Horne's interest in issues of aging began a decade ago with the clients and families who come to the adult daycare center in Milwaukee where she works with her husband, Larry Schmidt. Her writings on the subject began when she started to give care to her own parents in Virginia. She is the author of *Caregiving: Helping an Aging Loved One; Homesharing and Other Lifestyle Options* (co-authored with housing expert Leo Baldwin); and *The Nursing Home Handbook* (all published by AARP Books).

Horne has a master's degree in communication from the University of Cincinnati and is a 1988 Fellow of the Midwest Geriatric Education Center. Horne was also awarded a grant in 1989 from the Association of University Programs in Health Administration to develop a curriculum module on long-term care. Her personal experiences, combined with her professional expertise, have made her a popular speaker at conferences and seminars and a guest expert on national television and radio talk programs.

For Further Reading

Adams, Martha. *Alzheimer's Disease: A Call to Courage for Caregivers.* St. Meinrad, Ind: Abbey Press, 1987.

Anderson, Louie. *Dear Dad: Letters from an Adult Child.* New York: Penguin Books, 1991.

Bauer, Clare. *When I Grow Too Old to Dream: A Journal on Alzheimer's Disease.* Riverside, N.J.: Crestwood House, 1989.

Caroll, David L. *When Your Loved One Has Alzheimer's Disease.* New York: Harper and Row, 1990.

Ferdenberger, Herbert J. *Burn-Out: The High Cost of Achievement.* New York: Bantam Books, 1981.

Grollman, Earl A. *In Sickness and in Health.* Boston: Beacon Press, 1987.

Levy, Michael T. *Parenting Mom and Dad.* New York: Prentice Hall, 1991.

Martz, Sandra, ed. *When I Am an Old Woman I Shall Wear Purple.* Manhattan Beach, Calif.: Papier-Mache Press, 1988.

Paul, Jordan and Margaret. *Do I Have to Give Up Me to Be Loved by You?* Minneapolis: CompCare Publishers, 1983.

Pierskalla, Carol S., and Jane D. Heald. *Help for Families of the Aging: Caregivers Can Express Love and Set Limits.* Support Source, Swarthmore, Pa., 1988.

Silverstone, Barbara, and Helen Kandel Hyman. *You and Your Aging Parent.* New York: Pantheon Books, 1989.

Sommers, Tish, and Laurie Shields. *Women Take Care.* Gainesville, Fla.: Triad Publishing Company, 1987.